ITIL® v3 Foundations

A Time-Compressed Resource To Passing The ITIL® v3 Foundation Exam On Your 1st Attempt!

JASON DION

DISCLAIMER

While Dion Training Solutions, LLC takes care to ensure the accuracy and quality of these materials, we cannot guarantee their accuracy, and all materials are provided without any warranty whatsoever, including, but not limited to, the implied warranties of merchantability or fitness for a particular purpose. The name used in any data files provided with this course is that of a fictitious company and fictional employees. Any resemblance to current or future companies or employees is purely coincidental. If you believe we used your name or likeness accidentally, please notify us and we will change the name in the during next revision of the manuscript. Dion Training Solutions is an independent provider of integrated training solutions for individuals, businesses, educational institutions, and government agencies. The use of screenshots, photographs of another entity's products, or another entity's product name or service in this book is for editorial purposes only. No such use should be construed to imply sponsorship or endorsement of this book by nor any affiliation of such entity with Dion Training Solutions. This book may contain links to sites on the Internet that are owned and operated by third parties (the "External Sites"). Dion Training Solutions is not responsible for the availability of, or the content located on or through, any External Site. Please contact Dion Training Solutions if you have any concerns regarding such links or External Sites. Any screenshots used are for illustrative purposes are the intellectual property of the original software owner.

TRADEMARK NOTICES

ITIL® is a registered trademark of Axelos Limited in the United States and other countries. All other product and service names used may be common law or registered trademarks of their respective proprietors.

PIRACY NOTICES

This book conveys no rights in the software or other products about which it was written; all use or licensing of such software or other products is the responsibility of the user according to terms and conditions of the software owner. Do not make illegal copies of books or software. If you believe that this book, related materials, or any other Dion Training Solutions materials are being reproduced or transmitted without permission, please email us at piracy@diontraining.com.

ASIN: B074D6J1Q5
ISBN: 9781521969663

DEDICATION

To my loving wife and best friend, Tamera, for all her love and support during my many adventures while working in the IT Service Management industry, as well as during the time I worked on this manuscript.

And to my beloved children, Natalie and Jay Jay, thank you for your patience while I worked many a late night laying the foundation upon which this book is built.

CONTENTS

ACKNOWLEDGEMENTS

I blame all my previous students for my writing this book. In every class I have taught, there has been at least one student asking, *When are you going to write a book about all this stuff,* and so here we are today. Writing this book has been an interesting experience, as well as a challenging one. But, in all seriousness, this book is written for all my students, in the classroom, online, and around the world. Thank you all for your encouragement and probing, without you this book wouldn't exist.

I hope that you all find great value in the method to my madness as we work together to conquer the ITIL® v3 Foundation certification exam on your first attempt!

Chapter 1
INTRODUCTION

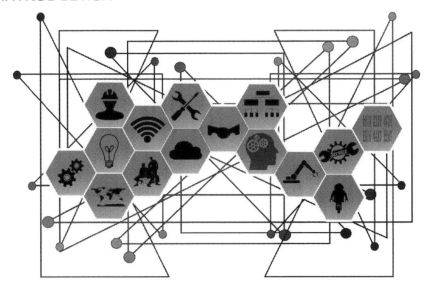

OBJECTIVES

- Understand how this book is designed to help you pass your certification exam quickly
- Understand how the exam is designed and how to take the certification exam
- Understand some tips and tricks for conquering the ITIL® v3 Foundation exam

Welcome to Information Technology Infrastructure Library (ITIL®) v3 Foundations: Cram to Pass. In this book, you will receive a crash course that will introduce you to everything you need to know in order to pass the ITIL® v3 Foundation certification exam. This book covers just the essentials with no fluff, filler, or extra material, so you can learn the material quickly and conquer the certification exam with ease.

This book assumes that you have no previous experience with the ITIL® v3 framework and will teach you the bare minimum you need to know in order to take and pass the ITIL® v3 Foundation certification exam on your first attempt.

This book will NOT teach you everything you need to know to be efficient or effective in implementing the ITIL® v3 Framework in your organization. This text is designed to get you to pass the certification exam, not to make you an expert in ITIL®.

Due to the design of this text, we will move at a very quick pace through the material. If you read this entire book and take the practice exams located at the end of the text (scoring at least an 85% or higher), you will be ready to take and pass the ITIL® v3 Foundation certification exam on your first attempt!

EXAM BASICS

The ITIL® v3 Foundation certification exam is an entry-level certification for Information Technology personnel interested in the Information Technology Service Management (ITSM) discipline. This foundational certification covers a general awareness of the elements, concepts, and terminology used in the ITIL® Service Lifecycle and IT Service Management.

The target audience for the ITIL® v3 Foundation certification is:

- People requiring an understanding of the ITIL® framework
- People needing an understanding of how ITIL® can enhance IT service management within an organization
- IT professionals in organizations that adopted ITIL® and need to understand ongoing service improvement

The certification exam consists of 40 multiple-choice questions which must be completed within 60 minutes. A minimum score of 26 out of 40 questions is required to pass the certification exam, equating to a score of 65% or higher. The exam is a closed book exam, with no notes or study materials being allowed to be used during your examination.

As of January 1, 2018, PeopleCert has been granted the exclusive rights to conduct the examination of all candidates for the ITIL® Foundation certification. You must sign up through their website located at https://www.PeopleCert.org. The exam is conducting over the Internet, allowing you to sit for the exam in the comfort of their own home or office.

The current cost of the exam as of the publication of this book is between $300-350 USD, as PeopleCert has been utilizing variable pricing based on factors such as demand for the certification, the country of the examination candidate, and more.

EXAM TIPS AND TRICKS

Before we dig into the content of the ITIL® v3 Foundation exam, it is important for you to read through some exam tips and tricks. This will help you understand exactly how to study for the exam as you read through the rest of this book and will help you to focus your efforts to get the most out of this material.

The most important thing to remember when taking the ITIL® v3 Foundation exam is that there will be no trick questions come test day. Every question is precisely worded to match the material you have studied. You should read the questions multiple times to ensure you understand exactly what the question is asking you, and that you are answering the question being asked. Anytime you see the words ALWAYS or NEVER in an answer, think twice about selecting it. In Information Technology Service Management (ITSM), rarely is there a case where something ALWAYS or NEVER applies to a given situation!

As you read the questions and answers, always be on the lookout for distractors or red herrings. Generally, there is at least one listed in the possible answer choices to try and distract you.

If you see a question with bold, italics, or in all uppercase, you should pay close attention to those words because the test writers have decided that those are keywords that are very important to selecting the correct answer.

It is important to remember what things in the ITIL® v3 Framework are processes and which are functions. We will cover both throughout this book. If a question asks about a process, make sure you don't select an answer that contains a function or a service.

Also remember that you must answer the questions based on your ITIL® knowledge and studies from this textbook, not your personal workplace experience. Your workplace may not be implementing ITIL® correctly in their IT Service Management operations, so you must always select the book answer when answering a question on the exam.

Remember that on exam day, you should select the BEST answer. Each question may have several right answers, but one is always the *most* right answer. When in doubt, choose the answer that is correct in the most number of situations!

On test day, you don't have to memorize the definitions from the ITIL® v3 Framework word for word, but you must be able to recognize them from the choices given. This is an essential difference in IT Certification testing, where the answers are multiple-choice, and the tests you may have taken in high school or college where you had to fill in a blank or write a short answer. In the IT Certification world, you must be able to recognize, not regurgitate, the information.

As you study the material in this book, keep these objectives in mind:
- Know generic process model and process characteristics
- Be able to differentiate between a service, process, and function

Finally, remember that if you get asked about the service or process, verify your answer matches the question asked. If the question asks about a process, DO NOT select an answer with the word service in it!

Chapter 2
ITSM AND THE ITIL® FRAMEWORK

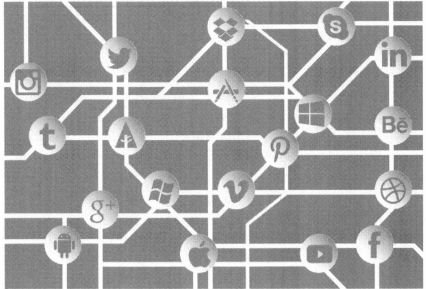

OBJECTIVES

- Understand ITSM and the fundamentals of the ITIL® v3 Framework
- Be able to name the 5 phases of the Service Lifecycle
- Understand the characteristics of processes in ITIL®
- Understand the characteristics of functions in ITIL®
- Understand the standard roles in ITIL®
- Understand organizational structures and their relation to ITIL®
- Understand the various types of service desks in ITIL®
- Understand the Technical Management function
- Understand the Application Management function
- Understand the IT Operations Management function
- Understand the RACI Model

IT Service Management (ITSM) is the complete set of activities required to provide value to a customer through services, including policies and strategies to Plan, Design,

Deliver, Operate, and Control IT services. This leads us to the question, what is the definition of a service. A Service is a means of delivering value to customers by facilitating the outcomes customers want to achieve without the ownership of specific costs and risk.

For example, if you own a company that wants to host a website, you would want the functionality of having a website up and running for your customers to access 24 hours a day, 7 days a week. But, you may not want the expense involved in buying the servers, paying the IT personnel to run those servers, and all the other associated costs. So, instead, you can pay a service provider to run your website for a monthly fee. You, as a customer, have now received the outcome you wanted without the ownership of the specific costs or risks.

There are many different IT Service Management models and frameworks in the industry, but we are only going to focus on one: ITIL®. The Information Technology Infrastructure Library (ITIL®) was developed as a framework for organizations to use in order to perform ITSM. Not surprisingly, on the ITIL® v3 Foundation certification exam, the only ITSM framework that is tested is the ITIL® v3 framework. For that reason, this book will only focus on the ITIL® v3 processes and functions.

The ITIL® framework is made up of the best practices from throughout the IT industry. Best practices are proven activities or processes that have been successfully used by many different organizations in a specific industry. These best practices come from multiple sources, including standards, industry practices, academic research, training and education, and internal employee experiences.

THE SERVICE LIFECYCLE

The ITIL® v3 Framework is built around the Service Lifecycle. This lifecycle consists of 5 phases: Service Strategy, Service Design, Service Transition, Service Operation, and Continual

Service Improvement. There are many ways to visualize these five phases and how they work together. The official ITIL® v3 Framework materials like to depict it as follows:

While this lifecycle diagram is useful, it doesn't really depict the reality of the ITIL® v3 Service Lifecycle as it is used in the *real-world*. Instead, I prefer to diagram the lifecycle with a continuously feedback loop, as shown in this modified lifecycle diagram:

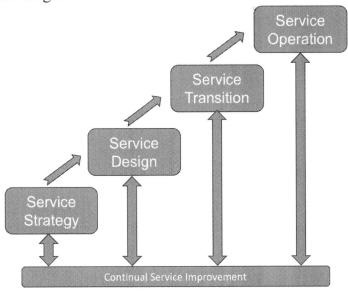

As shown in the lifecycle diagram, each service begins its life in Service Strategy, then moves up and to the right from phase to phase in the lifecycle. At each and every point, there is a continuous feedback opportunity to the Continual Service Improvement phase, where those changes can be implemented in earlier stages (for the next version of a given service). This really captures the idea of Continual Service Improvement more clearly, and more closely reflects the reality you will experience in the *real-world* IT Service Management.

Each phase of this service lifecycle will be covered in-depth in subsequent chapters of this book. As we cover each phase, we will also cover its associated processes and functions to ensure you are ready for those questions on exam day.

PROCESSES

A **process** is a set of coordinated activities that combine resources and capability to produce an outcome that creates value for the customer. In the ITIL® v3 Framework, there are 26 distinct processes covered throughout the 5 phases of the service lifecycle. But, only 22 of these processes are covered in-depth by the Foundation exam.

Each and every process has to have the same four characteristics. First, they must respond to a specific event, called a *trigger*. Second, they must be *measurable* by using metrics like performance, cost, productivity, quality, and duration. Third, they must produce a *specific result*. Finally, they must deliver a result to a *defined customer* to meet expectations.

In the summary chart on the next page, you will see a complete list of all the processes and functions covered on the ITIL® v3 Foundation exam. Each of these processes and functions will be covered in-depth later in this book as we cover each of the service lifecycle phases in their own chapters.

ITILv3: Overview of Processes & Phases

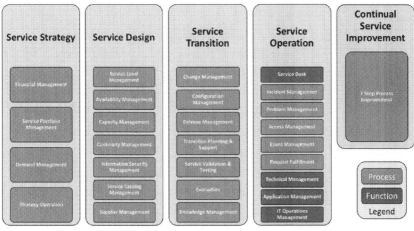

Each process can be depicted using a three-layered model containing its process control, the process itself, and the process enablers. The process controls include process policies, ownership, documentation, review programs, etc. The process itself contains the steps of the process, procedures, work instructions, roles, triggers, metrics, inputs, and outputs. The process enablers include resources and capabilities that are required to support the process.

Three-Layered Model of a Process

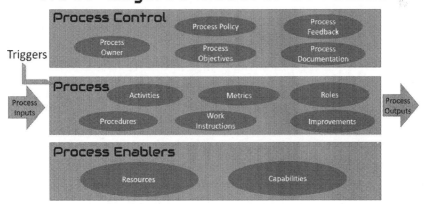

FUNCTIONS

Functions are self-contained units of an organization specialized to perform specific tasks and are responsible for an outcome. These functions actually perform the activities of processes. Functions consist of a group of people and the tools they use to create a given outcome through a process.

So, to clarify, what makes a process different than a function? Processes help organizations achieve certain objectives, even across multiple functional groups. Functions, on the other hand, add stability and structure to the organization by being mapped to the organizational chart, having a budget tied to them, and even having defined reporting structures associated with them.

Processes rely on functions to accomplish their outcomes. In fact, many times, processes rely on multiple functions to accomplish their outcomes. Processes and functions are both very intertwined, and processes would not be effective without supporting functions. Additionally, both processes and functions have roles associated with them, which we will cover in the next section.

ROLES

Roles are a collection of specific responsibilities, duties, or positions within a process or function. Each role can be held by an individual or team of individuals. Additionally, a single person or team can have more than one role. In the ITIL® v3 Framework, there are four standard roles that are utilized: service owner, process owner, service manager, and process manager.

The **service owner** is accountable for the overall design, performance, integration, improvement, and management of a single service. They are responsible for:

- Initiation, transition, and maintaining of the service
- Ensuring service delivery is met

- Identifying service improvements
- Being the liaison to the Process Owners
- Reporting and monitoring
- Overall accountability for delivering the service

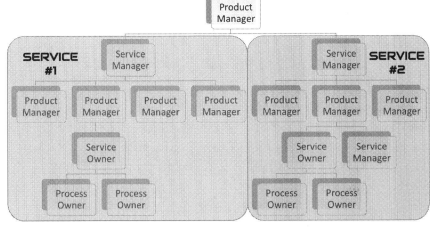

The **process owner** is accountable for the overall design, performance, integration, improvement, and management of a single process. They are responsible for:

- Initiation, transition, and maintaining of the process
- Defining the process strategy and policy
- Assisting in the process design
- Ensuring the process is documented
- Auditing the process for efficiency
- Communicating the process to others
- Provisioning resources and training
- Inputting suggestions into the service improvement program

The **service manager** is accountable for the development, performance, and improvement of all services.

The **process manager** is accountable for the development, performance, and improvement of all processes.

There are two additional roles that are not considered part of the standard roles: the product manager and the process practitioner. The **product manager** is accountable for the development, performance, and improvement of a group of related services. The **process practitioner** is responsible for actually conducting the actions and functions associated with operating the service. For example, the person answering the phones in the service desk may be considered a process practitioner for the Service Request Fulfillment process.

ORGANIZATIONAL STRUCTURE

One of the most common questions I have been asked by management when they are looking to adopt the ITIL® v3 Framework in their organization is "How should we organize our workforce to support ITIL®?" Well, this is exactly the wrong question to be asking, because ITIL® does not provide a model for how to structure your organization!

Instead, the ITIL® v3 Framework provides some useful guidance on organizational structure, but none of it is to be considered prescriptive in nature. In fact, each volume of the ITIL® v3 Framework manuals has as its 6th chapter, guidance on organizational structure. Just open up any of the manuals (Service Strategy, Service Design, Service Transition, Service Operations, or Continual Service Improvement), and you will find Chapter 6 as "Organizing for _____".

In these chapters, you will find numerous roles and responsibilities listed. But, you should use these as more of a checklist to see if you have considered the roles, not as a requirement to create all of those roles in your own organization.

So, if ITIL® v3 doesn't dictates organizational structure, what should you be concerned with when it comes to this topic? There are a few key concepts here to remember. First, roles can be filled by multiple people, and one person could fill many different roles. If there are many people filling a given role, you need to ensure there are no gaps or seams in their job responsibilities, or else things could "fall through the cracks".

Always ensure that all roles required are filled by someone inside your organization.

ITIL® focuses on the relationships between functions and processes, and between the four standard roles. Much of the focus in ITIL® is placed on the four major functions that support the various processes: Service Desk, Technical Management, Application Management, and IT Operations Management.

SERVICE DESK

The **service desk** provides a single, central point of contact for all users of IT services. The is the first point of contact for all issues with all services, including inbound incidents, service requests, change requests, and much more. Usually, the service desk also owns the Incident Management process, since they are the first call by a customer when something goes wrong with a given service.

Many organizations have a help desk while others have a service desk, but what is the difference? Well, the first service desks were simply call centers or help desks. These help desks really focused on answering customer calls and fixing broken services for the customers. Over time, these help desks became better organized and evolved into full-blown service desks, offering more than just a "break-fix" mentality to problem solving. These service desks became the singular point of focus for customers, handling break-fix issues, upgrades, training, and much more.

There are four major types of service desk models: Local Service Desk, Centralized Service Desk, Virtual Service Desk, and Follow-the-Sun.

The **local service desk** is physically located close to the customers they support. Usually, they reside in the same building or offices as their customers, such as an embedded IT support person inside the accounting department, or even a singular service desk to support the entire building.

The **centralized service desk** model makes better use of resources, improves consistency, and centralizes management. Under this model, a single service desk would remotely answer all telephone support calls, regardless of the location of the customer.

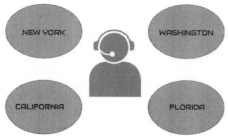

The **virtualized service desk** doesn't require a centralized location, but can still make better use of resources, improves consistency, and centralizes management. Under this model, the location of the service desk personnel is irrelevant and could even include remote home-based teleworkers. Customers simply call a centralized telephone support number and their call is routed to the next available agent, regardless of the customer's or agent's location.

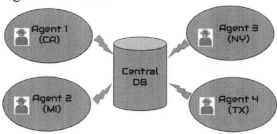

The **follow-the-sun** service desk model combines local, centralized, and virtual service desks, allowing for 24x7 coverage across all time zones. As shown in the image, during the normal business hours the calls are routed to a call center in that time zone (for example, a New York support desk during office hours in the United States). If a United States customer calls for service after normal business hours, their call is routed to a different call center based on the normal working hours of those service desk locations.

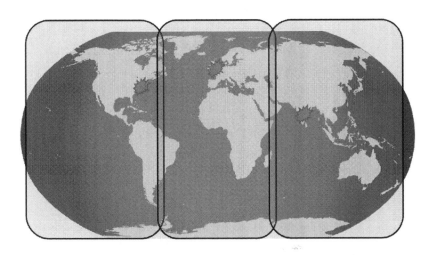

TECHNICAL MANAGEMENT

The **technical management** function is responsible for the procurement, development, and management of the technical skill sets and resources required to support the infrastructure and the ITSM efforts. This function provides technical resources to all phases of the ITIL® v3 Lifecycle. The technical management function ensures that the Service Provider has the right skill sets available to deliver the services it offers to its customers. Generally, technical management is divided into specialty areas, such as networking, security, databases, storage, servers, and other specialized fields required to support the overall service provider objectives.

APPLICATION MANAGEMENT

The **application management** function provides end-to-end management of applications in the environment, and involves cultivating the skill sets and resources to support all phases of the lifecycle. Application management also helps to identify software requirements and their sourcing (internal/external).

Application management is focused on the ongoing oversight, operational management, and improvement of applications for both utility and warranty. **Application development**, on the other hand, is focused on design and construction of an application solution to gain initial utility.

Application management is a function that supports and does not replace other core processes, such as Incident Management, Problem Management, Change Management, Availability Management, and many others.

IT OPERATIONS MANAGEMENT

The **IT Operations Management** function provides a stable platform on which services can be delivered to meet the agreed-upon business needs. It performs the day-to-day running of the IT infrastructure and the facilities that house that infrastructure. IT Operations Management split into two sub-functions: Operations Control and Facilities Management.

Operations Control monitors the infrastructure for optimal performance minute-by-minute and conducts the normal maintenance cycles required. To do this, operations controls performs Console Management, backup and restoral operations, media management, batch job execution, and more. These operations are usually controlled from the Network Operations Center (NOC) or the Operations Bridge. In this example, an Operations Bridge is being used to monitor local traffic conditions, as well as the automated systems that help to alleviate them like using traffic cameras and stoplights.

Photo by: Highway's Agency (2011)

Unlike Operations Control, **Facilities Management** is only concerned with physical environment of the IT infrastructure, including the power, cooling, fire suppression, and physical access to the data centers and server rooms. To be effective, though, the facilities management team must have a close working relationship with the Operations Control watch team. In many organizations, both the Operations Control and Facilities Management personnel are collocated in the same workspaces.

THE RACI MODEL

The **RACI Model** is a generic tool for reviewing and assigning four key roles to any activity: Responsible, Accountable, Consulted, and Informed. Each activity can have many roles who are responsible, consulted, and informed, but only one role can be listed as accountable. As the old saying goes, *if everyone is accountable, then nobody is accountable!*

The RACI Model provides a visual indication of the linkages between roles, their responsibility, and the accountability for a given task in a process. **Responsible** (R) refers to the person who executes or performs the activity. **Accountable** (A) refers to the person who owns the activity and must answer for its outcomes. Only a single person can be held accountable for a given activity. **Consulted** (C) refers to the person who reviews and provides advice and authorization for the activity. **Informed** (I) refers to the person who receives updates on activity's progress.

A simplified version of a Responsible, Accountable, Consulted, and Informed (RACI) Matrix for the Incident Matrix Process is provided as an example:

Incident Management Process			
	End User	Service Desk Analyst	Incident Response Team
Detect	R	I	R, I, C
Log	C	R	R, A
Categorize	C	R	R, A
Investigate	C	R, I	R, A

- Responsible
- Accountable
- Consulted
- Informed

Chapter 3
SERVICE STRATEGY PHASE

OBJECTIVES

- Describe and understand the Service Strategy phase
- Describe a business case analysis
- Describe value, utility, and warranty
- Describe service assets
- Describe the Service Portfolio Management process
- Describe the Strategy Management process
- Describe the Demand Management Process
- Describe the Financial Management Process

The **Service Strategy** phase establishes and manages the broadest policies and standards to govern how a service provider will operate. This will determine the selection of services a service provider will offer to its customers. All services should deliver value to customers, enable the service providers to capture value, be of acceptable cost to the service provider, and be of acceptable risk to the service provider.

In the last chapter, a service was defined as a means of providing value to customers by facilitating the outcomes they want to achieve without the ownership of specific costs and risks. Now, the Service Strategy phase aims to creates value to the service provider and its customer by offering services that are aligned with business objectives and are likely to offer value. Also, these services should allow for customers to be charged for their use or give the service provider another beneficial (non-monetary) outcome. At the end of the day, the service provider must be able to handle the costs and risks associated with offering the service, otherwise they could go out of business.

In the Service Strategy phase, there are four processes we must learn: Service Portfolio Management, Strategy Management (also called Strategy Operations), Financial Management, and Demand Management.

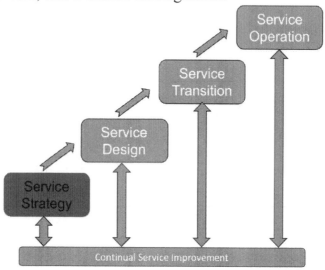

BUSINESS CASE ANALYSIS

A **business case analysis** is a structured and documented justification for a new investment that argues the benefits and costs of a particular service. Each time you create a new or changing service, you should create a business case analysis to determine the expected Return on Investment (ROI) for the service.

There are five parts to a business case analysis: introduction, methods and assumptions, business impacts, risks and contingencies, and recommendations. Each business case analysis will make a case for a new or changed service based on either its return on investment (ROI) or value on investment (VOI). The **return on investment** (ROI) is the expected financial growth created by a service; or more simply, the amount of money returned to the service provider after its costs of providing a given service. The **value on investment** (VOI) is the expected non-financial return created by a service, such as in a service provider's increased recognition or reputation.

VALUE, UTILITY, AND WARRANTY

Value is created from the balance between utility and warranty. A service must have both utility and warranty in order to create value for a customer.

The **utility** of a service is its *fit for purpose*. This refers to the functionality of a service or its ability to enable a job to be done. Utility is important because it removes the constraints faced by a customer, or increases the customer's overall performance through a given service.

The **warranty** of a service is its *fit for use*. This refers to the mix of availability, capacity, continuity, and security of a given service. While utility sells services, without warranty a service will fail to operate and create issues for your customers.

To create maximum value, you attempt to find the perfect balance to create the most value. Neither utility nor warranty are always more important, it is always dependent on the customer requirements and the service being provided. To have value, though, you must have at least some amount of utility and warranty, as shown in the diagram. Customers want services that are fit for purpose AND fit for use.

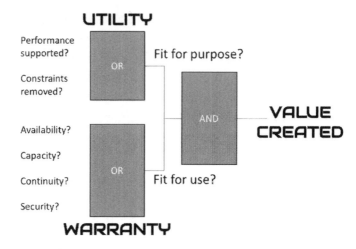

In the graphics below, there are three examples of value as a balance of utility and warranty.

In the first example, we have poor value because we have a website that was created with all the latest technology and the best features (high utility). The infrastructure, however, was built poorly and results in limited bandwidth to support the site (poor warranty). This thereby creates poor overall value to the customer.

In the second example, we have another example of poor value to the customer. In this example, the database designer created a horribly inefficient design that doesn't meet all the customer's needs (low utility). The infrastructure, though, was built with a highly redundant and available backbone (creating high warranty). As shown in the graphic, the overall result is poor value to the customer.

In the third example, we see a good balance of utility and warranty, resulting in a maximum value for the customer. This is the perfect balance we seek to achieve, with the optimal amount of utility (fit for purpose) and warrant (fit for use).

Every time a service is added or changed, it is important to consider the utility and warranty of that service. Remember, while utility *sells* services, it is the warranty that really requires the resources to support the service, and therefore represents an increase in costs.

SERVICE ASSETS

Service assets are resources and capabilities which the service provider must allocate to provide a given service.

Resources are tangible items that contribute to a service. Items such as raw materials, infrastructure, applications, information, and even people (labor) can be purchased with financial capital, making them tangible items according to the ITIL® framework.

Capabilities are specialized skills or abilities that are applied by organization to add value. These are the intangibles of a company, such as its management, organization, processes, and skills.

SERVICE PORTFOLIO MANAGEMENT PROCESS

The **Service Portfolio Management Process** is concerned with managing the services that comprise the service portfolio. This is where services are organized, identified, described, evaluated, selected, and charted; as well as their place in the service portfolio.

The **service portfolio** is the complete set of services under management by a service provider. The service portfolio is comprised of three major sections: the service pipeline, service catalog, and retired services

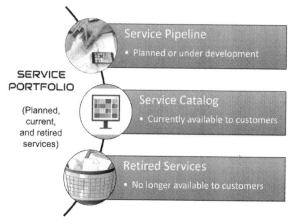

The service portfolio's purpose is to help the service provider understand how its resources are used to maximize value. All resources are allocated to services throughout their lifecycle from the IT director's resource pool. As services move into the Service Operation phase, they will usually use more resource than they did in earlier stages. In fact, many services use over 70% of their resources and budget just in the Service Operations phase!

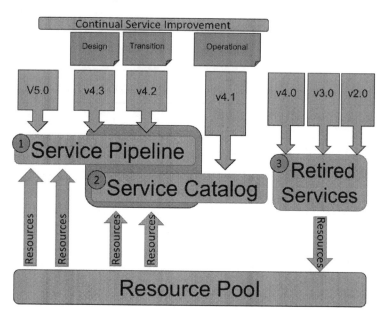

STRATEGY MANAGEMENT PROCESS

The **Strategy Management Process** ensures a service strategy is defined, maintained, and managed. This process focuses on the development of service concepts in preparation for selection of services to be provided. In some ITIL® books, this process is also called the Strategy Operation Process.

In the Strategy Management Process, there are several key activities that occur. First, the organization seeks to understand the current marketplace. They do this by asking questions such as "who is the customer", "what do they value", and "how does the customer define value". Next, the offerings and services are developed by asking questions such as "what services could be offered to provide value to our customers" and "how can we offer a unique or distinctive value in the marketplace".

During this process, strategic assets are also developed by determining the appropriate resources and capabilities to apply to the proposed service. To best determine this, questions are asked, such as "what resources would be required to offer the proposed service" and "what capabilities would be needed to provide the service".

Finally, the service execution is prepared for by outlining the broad scope of the service's objectives. The specific questions considered during this activity is things like "how can we prepare to develop the service", "what are the service objectives", and "what critical success factors must be met to achieve our objectives". During Service Design, this broad scope is further defined and narrowed as the service is designed more fully.

DEMAND MANAGEMENT PROCESS

The **Demand Management Process** is used to identify the demand for a particular service to prevent capacity limitations. It is imperative to understand your customer's demand on your services because unmanaged demand is a cost and risk to the service provider. For example, if you planned to support 1,000 website visitors per day using 1 Mb of data, but instead you had a large surge in demand. Now, you have 100,000 web visitors per day and they are using over 1 Gb of data. The worst case may be if you are hosting your website on a small virtualized server because you may experience a failure in service as the server cannot handle the increased load of all those new visitors. Under the best-case scenario, you may have built your service to run elastically using a cloud-based architecture like Amazon Web Services or Microsoft's Azure platform, in which case you may only face cost and budget overruns for excessive bandwidth utilization under their fee for service model. Either way, this unmanaged demand is becoming a realized risk to your organization.

During the Demand Management Process, the patterns of business activity are identified and analyzed. This analysis of the service utilization helps determine the different types of users and their patterns. Using these patterns of activity, user profiles are identified and documented for your customers, and help us to better predict future demand on the service.

Understanding the patterns of business activity is extremely important, because businesses always have busy and slow periods. If a service is built to handle the peak load, it may be underutilized during the majority of the year, costing the company resources to maintain the unused capability. Consider the time period of November and December. If you are running a retail website, you may experience excessively high demand during the holiday buying season. But, if you are a training and education company, you may see a sharp decline in your demand during this same period, as people are focused on holiday shopping and their winter vacations. If you don't account for peaks and valleys in your demand curve, you will be unable to provide efficient service which will lead to unnecessary additional costs in delivery your services.

FINANCIAL MANAGEMENT PROCESS

The **Financial Management Process** is used to understand and manage financial resources, costs, and opportunities for a service. Proper financial management helps to provide and organization with a clear method of generating data to aid in management decisions.

One of the most important functions of the financial management process is to secure funding to design, develop, and deliver services to support business processes and to ensure service provider doesn't promise what they cannot deliver. Financial management is all about maintaining a balance of cost and quality, as well as a balance of supply and demand.

There are three major activities in the financial management: budgeting, accounting, and charging.

Budgeting is the forecasting and planning of how to spend money in relation to providing a service.

Accounting is the tracking of money by cost centers and against the original budget.

Charging is how an organization gets payment from the customers for services. Remember, with charging, it doesn't have to refer to an external customer. Some organizations require departments to reimburse other departments on a *fee for service* model by using charging against the serviced departments budget to offset the costs incurred by the servicing department.

I previously held a position as the IT Director for an organization that had previously never had an IT department. This organization was actually quite large (several thousand people), but each department handled their own IT services. When I was brought onboard as the IT Director, my job was to consolidate all the IT services under one department, the new IT department. The challenge, though, was that the executive level of the organization never set aside a budget to support the new IT department.

Since the yearly budget was finalized for all of the other departments, I recommended the IT department operate under a charging model called "fee-for-service". In this model, my department would charge the other departments whenever they utilized our IT services.

For example, when a sales department employee called the Service Desk, a charge was accounted for and money was moved from the sales department's account into the IT department's account. If someone wanted a new printer, we would order it, install it, and service it, but there was a cost charged back against their line of accounting.

By doing this, the actual cost of IT was able to be realized by the different department managers, and the executive level was able to better understand exactly how much IT was costing the organization. We used the charging model for about 2 years while we migrated everything into the new centralized IT department. During that time, we were able to determine the correct budget for the IT department to request, and once authorized we were able to migrate away from the charging model for the majority of our services.

Chapter 4
SERVICE DESIGN PHASE

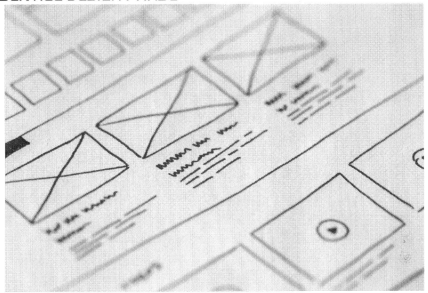

OBJECTIVES

- Describe and understand the Service Design phase
- Describe a business value in terms of service design
- Describe quality in service design
- Describe the 4 P's of service design
- Describe the Service Catalog Management Process
- Describe the Service Catalog types
- Describe the Service Level Management Process
- Describe the Availability Management Process
- Describe the Capacity Management Process
- Describe the Information Security Management Process
- Describe the Supplier Management Process

The **Service Design** phase conducts the detailed planning of the service and all supporting materials to allow it into the live environment. During this phase, the following questions are answered:

- How will the service be supported?

- How will the service be tested?
- How will the future development of the service occur?

By the end of the Service Design phase, a Service Design Plan is created and passed to the Service Transition team. This Service Design Plan should be a detailed, comprehensive, well communicated plan that is agreed upon by all the stakeholders. This plan is a blueprint of the service that includes the component of the service, identification of any resources that may be shared with another existing service, a test plan, a support plan, and a future development plan.

In Service Design, the organization is concerned with creating an effective, but not necessarily efficient, service. Over time, and through the Continual Service Improvement process, the service will become more and more efficient. For the time being, though, the organization is looking for a service that meets the objectives in same manner (has sufficiently good utility), even if it isn't the most cost effective or efficient solution.

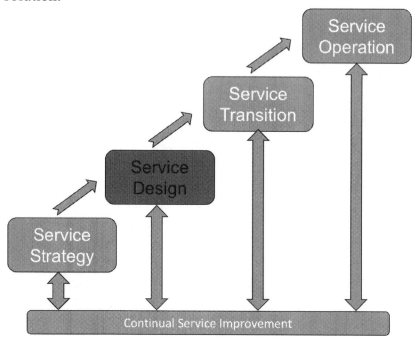

When performing Service Design, there are five aspects to consider. First, you must have considered the new or changed service itself. Second, consider what service Management processes are needed to support the service. Third, determine which service management systems and tools are needed to support the service. Fourth, define what technology architectures will be used by the service. Finally, create the measurement systems and metrics that will be utilized to understand the performance of the new or changed service.

In the Service Design phase, there are seven processes we must learn: Service Catalog Management, Service Level Management, Availability Management, Capacity Management, Continuity Management, Information Security Management, and Supplier Management.

BUSINESS VALUE IN SERVICE DESIGN

With all service designs, we must ensure that we are creating services that are aligned with business objectives in order to create maximum value. Each service should provide the agreed upon utility and warranty to meet objectives that were identified during the Service Strategy phase.

For a service to be effective and efficient over time, the organization must ensure that its service management processes are capable of supporting the service. If the organization's service management systems and tools do not support the proposed service offerings, then the overall value of the service to the business will suffer.

All services should be built to the agreed upon architectural standards and designed so that the performance of the service is adequately measured. By providing continuous measurements and metrics, a service can be quantifiably assessed as to its success or failure over time, which aids in the managements future decisions on whether to continue supporting the service or retire it.

QUALITY IN SERVICE DESIGN

In order to create the best services, quality must be considered early in the process. During the Service Design phase, it is important to consider the entire service holistically to ensure that a quality service is created and fielded. But, in order to develop a quality service, it is necessary to have clear specifications for what level of quality must be achieved. Throughout the design and fielding of the new or changed service, it is important to ensure that processes exist to ensure proper warranty (fit for use).

Many people feel that they can simply correct design errors later in the process. While this is true, it is much more difficult and much costlier to fix design flaws during the Service Transition or Service Operation phases of the lifecycle. It is always best to design quality in during the Service Design phase, because it will lead to higher quality in the Service Operation phase, where it really counts. Remember, once you are into the Service Operation phase, your customer is experiencing your service. You want that service to be high quality, so design it right the first time!

THE 4 P'S OF SERVICE DESIGN

When designing a service, there are four essential P's that you must consider: People, Processes, Products, and Partners.

People consists of the technical staff, users, customers, stakeholders, board executives, and many others. People need to be trained, managed, supervised, led, hired, fired, and convinced. People are essential to the ITIL® lifecycle.

Processes form the heart of the IT Infrastructure Library (ITIL®). In ITIL® v3 Lifecycle, there are 26 distinct processes that are utilized. During Service Design, it is important to consider the processes that a new service will interact and utilize.

Products are made up of other services, technology (hardware, software, etc.), and tools needed to support the services. These can be built in-house or procured externally.

Partners are people and organizations that help the service provider to provide excellent services. These include manufacturers, suppliers, vendors, and other businesses.

SERVICE CATALOG MANAGEMENT PROCESS

The **Service Catalog Management Process** involves management and control of the service catalog. The **service catalog** is a database or structured document with information about all live services, including those available for deployment, that it is widely available to those who are approved to access it. This enables all stakeholders to have a clear understanding of services provided to support the business objectives, and to create a list and definition of all services provided by the organization.

The service catalog contains a list of all features of the service, its usage guidelines, the methods for accessing the service, its pricing information (or if a costing method is utilized for the service), the key points of contact, and any Service Level Agreement requirements that have been agreed upon by the stakeholders.

There are numerous benefits to having a well-produced service catalog. First, it helps to identify services that would be good candidates to bundle in order to provide better solutions to your customers. It can inform customers of services that are available for use. It also can help the service staff understand their part in the business process. Another great benefit is that it can assist in managing a customer's expectations concerning services to be rolled out in the coming months. Finally, it publishes the key Service Level Agreement targets, which again helps with managing customer expectations.

While the service catalog is heavily used in the Service Operation phase of the lifecycle, it is originally created and changed during the Service Design phase. The catalog's structure are managed and its contents are modified during Service Design. It is during this phase that the catalog is checked to ensure it is complete, accurate, and its data is current. As the service is designed, any proposed changes to the catalog are checked and authorized. The real reason that the service catalog management occurs during Service Design is because much of the information and documentation for a service is created during this stage of the lifecycle and this is the same information that should be placed into the service catalog to aid in further support of the new or changed service.

There are four types of service catalogs covered by the ITIL® v3 Foundation exam: Simple Service, Business or Customer, Technical or Supporting, and Alternate Views.

A **Simple Service Catalog** is a simplified matrix of available services that includes comprehensive and accurate information.

SIMPLE SERVICE CATALOG

Service	Students	Instructors	Sales	Payroll
Web Browsing	X	X	X	X
E-Mail	X	X	X	X
Paycheck Printing				X
IT Service Desk	X	X	X	X

A **Business or Customer Service Catalog** identifies the business processes that are being supported by the services and detailed versions can include service hours, SLA info, and escalation paths.

BUSINESS OR CUSTOMER SERVICE CATALOG

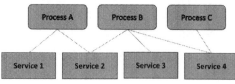

The **Technical or Supporting Service Catalog** provides another level of depth to the service catalog by covering infrastructure, applications, and outsourced services.

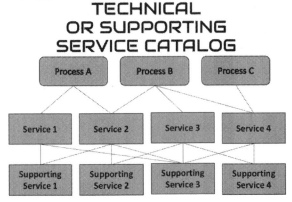

The **Alternate View Service Catalogs** can be displayed in various formats. For example, in a three-view model, the service catalog displays information relevant to the Technical or Supporting personnel, the retail customers, and the business-to-business customers.

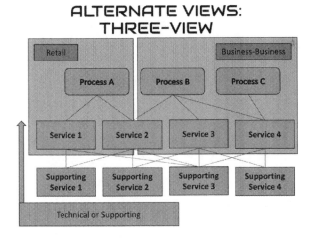

SERVICE LEVEL MANAGEMENT PROCESS

The Service Level Management Process secures and manages agreements between the service provider and the customer regarding the utility (level of performance) and warranty (level of reliability) of the service. Throughout this process, the service provider works with the customer to ensures all current and planned IT services can be delivered to agreed-upon service level targets, and that those service targets are able to be achieved and maintained.

During the Service Level Management Process, the following questions must be answered:

- What metrics are we collecting and comparing our performance to?
- What utility and warranty did you promise to your customers?
- Are your targets achievable and measurable?
- Are the targets relevant?

Service Level Management is achieved through a five-step process: Negotiate, Agree, Monitor, Report, and Review.

It is important to always keep the Service Level Management and Business Relationship Management processes aligned, as they are mutually supportive processes. In service level management, negotiation is always the key driver. Everything is negotiable in terms of service performance and service target levels, it is just a matter of justifying the cost associated with the given parameters.

Service Level Management is concerned with more than just a Service Level Agreement (SLA), though. This process also is responsible for the Operational Level Agreement (OLA) and the Underpinning Contract (UC).

A **Service Level Agreement** (SLA) is a written agreement between IT service provider and customer providing key service targets and responsibilities of both parties. It is a formal document, but not necessarily a legally binding contract. It should be written in clear, concise language that both parties agree upon. It is important to always monitor, report, and review the SLA targets to ensure they are being achieved.

An **Operational Level Agreement** (OLA) is an underpinning written agreement between two elements of the service provider organization regarding key service targets and responsibilities of both parties for the services being supported. This is similar to a SLA, but it is written between two internal departments within the service providers organization.

An **Underpinning Contract** (UC) is a legally binding agreement that conforms to contract law and organizational contract policy. It is written in "legalese" by a lawyer and is able to be held up in a court of law. These contracts are negotiated by the Supplier Management process.

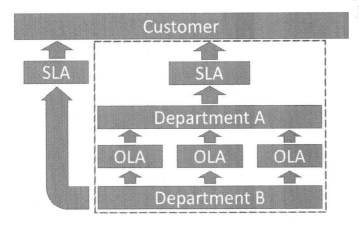

All of the SLAs, OLAs, and UCs must be kept in proper alignment to support the new or changed service, as well as the organizational business processes. This can get complicated as these various documents can become layered on top of one another to meet the given objectives.

The Service Level Management process is part of the Service Design process because it provides an opportunity to establish the performance requirements early in the service development to ensure the design work can be directed to meet the negotiated requirements for the service.

AVAILABILITY MANAGEMENT PROCESS

The **Availability Management Process** is concerned with meeting current and future availability needs of the business. It is responsible for ensuring that the level of availability delivered in all IT services meets the agreed availability needs and/or service level targets in a cost effective and timely manner.

Availability is the ability of a service, system, or configuration item to perform its function, when required. There are two types of availability: service availability and component availability. **Service availability** is focused on end-to-end service that is experienced by the end user or customer. **Component availability** is focused on each individual piece that together provides the end-to-end experience. So, which is more important?

If you are the end user of a service, then you don't really care as much about the component availability. As an end user, you are more focused on whether the end-to-end service is working properly when you need it. But, if you are the service provider, then you may become more concerned with the component availability.

If a power supply has failed, you may be at a loss of redundancy for that particular system. The end user may never notice that issue as a decline in performance, but you, as a service provider, know that you need to get it fixed quickly before your backup power supply fails. If both power supplies fail, then the service availability would be affected. So, it is all a matter of which perspective you are using as to which is more important to you: service availability or component availability.

The keys to successful availability management is to develop good service level targets for the availability portions of SLAs, to design services capable of meeting the agreed upon availability requirements, to measure and monitor availability of the services, and to be able to respond to incidents that detract from the overall availability of the services.

CAPACITY MANAGEMENT PROCESS

The **Capacity Management Process** is concerned with meeting current and future capacity and performance-related needs of the business. This process ensures that the capacity of IT services and the IT infrastructure meets the agreed capacity and performance-related requirements in a cost-effective and timely manner.

Capacity is the maximum throughput of a service, system, or configuration item. Capacity planning is conducted from the top-down beginning with business capacity management, then to service capacity management, and finally to the component capacity management.

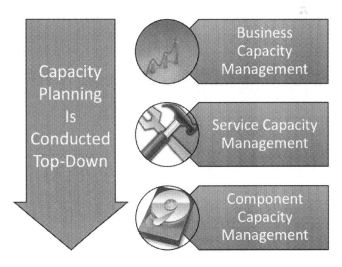

Business Capacity Management aligns capacity management to business plans and strategy. It translates requirements into services and infrastructure while coordinating with Business Relationship Management.

Service Capacity Management ensures services underpin the business processes and outcomes by focusing on end-to-end performance of operational services and workloads. Service capacity must be coordinated with the Service Portfolio Management process.

Component Capacity Management ensures an appropriate understanding of the technical components in the infrastructure by employing data analysis techniques to get maximum value from components. Component capacity must be coordinated with the Configuration Management process to ensure optimal configuration items are used for maximum efficiency and minimal cost.

The Capacity Management Process is responsible for creating the capacity plan for the organization. The capacity plan should include the details of the current and historic utilization level and performance, a forecast of the capacity changes needed to support future requirements, a list of assumptions used in the planning, and a costed list of recommendations for future implementation.

This capacity plan is used by the Information Technology (IT) Director to make service decisions. It is a continual balancing act for the IT Director between supply versus demand, as well as cost versus resources. The IT Director must consider if the current infrastructure can support a new or changed service, as well as if they must buy more infrastructure to support the new or changed service.

IT SERVICE CONTINUITY MANAGEMENT PROCESS

The **IT Service Continuity Management Process** is responsible for ensuring that the service provider can always provide the minimum agreed upon service levels by managing the risks associated with a disaster (or other incidents) that could seriously affect critical IT services.

Continuity management is all about the management of risk. Each risk analysis focuses on likely events and their impacts to the information technology operations and services provided. Continuity management focuses on the unlikely, but conceivable, events that could have a large impact on your services. Therefore, a contingency plan must be considered and made to cover these unlikely events. For each event, a business impact analysis (BIA) is conducted to better inform the IT Service Continuity plan.

How does IT Service Continuity Management differ from Availability Management, though? If an event is low impact or highly likely to occur, it is covered by Availability Management. For example, there is a high likelihood that a power supply on a server could fail, therefore the Availability Management process should have planned for a backup power supply or chosen servers with redundant power supplies to prevent this from having a negative impact to the services provided.

	Low Impact	High Impact
High Likelihood	Availability Management	Availability Management
Low Likelihood	Availability Management	IT Service Continuity Management

Instead, though, if we consider a high impact, low likelihood event such as a tornado destroying our data center, we would plan for this event through the IT Service Continuity Management process. In this case, we may plan to have offsite backups of our data or a second redundant data center located in a different part of the state or country. There are many ways to plan for recovery after a disaster, all of which are beyond the scope of the ITIL® v3 Foundation exam, but the idea that a disaster is planned for under the IT Service Continuity Management process is important to remember for the exam.

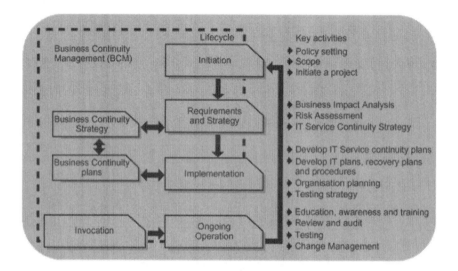

INFORMATION SECURITY MANAGEMENT PROCESS

The **Information Security Management Process** aligns IT security with business security in order to ensure the IT security aspects match agreed-upon needs of the business by protecting IT assets and services from security threats. It should fit into the organization's larger security management efforts. Under this process, the IT Security Policy for the organization is developed and managed. This policy is then used by the Access Management process during Service Operations.

Information security is always focused on three key principles: Confidentiality, Integrity, and Availability.

Confidentiality ensures only those with a "need to know" can access the information system or data held by the system. This is most often accomplished using encryption of the data.

Integrity ensures that the data and services are complete, accurate, and unmodified. This is most often accomplished by performing hashing of the data.

Availability ensures the customer can actually access the data they are authorized to access when needed. This is most often accomplished by creating redundancy in the services and systems.

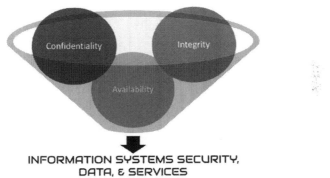

INFORMATION SYSTEMS SECURITY, DATA, & SERVICES

It is a balancing act to create a secure system that has confidentiality, integrity, and availability. As security increases, it becomes more difficult for the users of the system to accomplish their goals and operations can suffer. Just like the balancing act between utility and warranty, we must carefully balance the security of the service and the operations of the service.

SECURITY VS. OPERATIONS

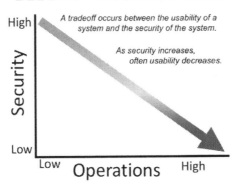

When it comes to Information Security Management, you must remember that while you can outsource a service, you can never outsource your responsibility for its security and data protection. If you outsource things to a third party, ensure the contract specifies they are still responsible for following your organization's IT Security policies. If you wish to dig deeper and learn more about Information Systems Management, you should review the international standard (**ISO 27000**). You will not be required to know further details about the Information Security Management Process for the ITIL Foundation exam beyond what was covered in this section, though.

SUPPLIER MANAGEMENT PROCESS

The **Supplier Management Process** is responsible for obtaining quality service from suppliers that provides fiscal value to meet the agreed upon needs of the business and ensures suppliers meet their contractual obligations. As the organization spends money with third-party suppliers, this process attempts to ensure value is obtained for that capital expense.

The Supplier Management Process is similar to the Service Level Management process, but it is concerned with external suppliers instead of internal suppliers and customers. Many organizations rely on external suppliers in order to provide their own services to their customers. There are four categories of suppliers: Strategic, Operational, Tactical, and Commodity.

Strategic Suppliers involve senior managers and sharing of confidential long-term plans between the organization and the supplier. This would be useful, for example, if you are a service provider that is looking to roll-out of a new nationwide fiber optic network, because the supplier will need to know your long-term plans to support your objectives.

Operational Suppliers involve the supply of operational services, such as the hosting a minor service or website for an organization.

Tactical Suppliers involve significant commercial activity and business interaction, for example if you hired a supplier to conduct your generator maintenance every month.

Commodity Suppliers involve the provisioning of low-value products, such as a supplier who provides your organization with the ink for your printers or your bathroom supplies.

Chapter 5
SERVICE TRANSITION PHASE

OBJECTIVES

- Describe and understand the Service Transition phase
- Describe the Service V-Model in the Service Transition phase
- Describe the Change Management Process
- Describe the Release and Deployment Management Process
- Describe the Service Asset and Configuration Management Process
- Describe the Service Validation and Testing Process
- Describe the Transition Planning and Support Process
- Describe the Evaluation Process
- Describe the Knowledge Management Process

The **Service Transition** phase conducts the management of change, and more specifically is focused on the introduction of new and changed services into the live environment. During this phase, things are actually purchased, installed, configured, tested, launched, and operated.

The Service Transition phase creates value to the business by enabling business change, while minimizing impact to the business that might otherwise result from unmanaged change. It enables the business to make use of new and changed services and ensures that the designs for services are implemented as intended. During this phase, the Service Management organization is prepared to support new and changed services and testing/validation occurs to reducing the number of defects introduced into the live environment.

By the end of the Service Transition phase, the physical development and implementation of a service is performed, the service is thoroughly tested and fielded into a live environment with no shortcomings identified, the configuration of the service is documented, and the operations personnel have been trained and are ready to support the new service.

In the Service Transition phase, there are seven processes we must learn: Change Management, Release and Deployment Management, Service Asset and Configuration Management, Service Validation and Testing, Transition Planning and Support, Evaluation, and Knowledge Management.

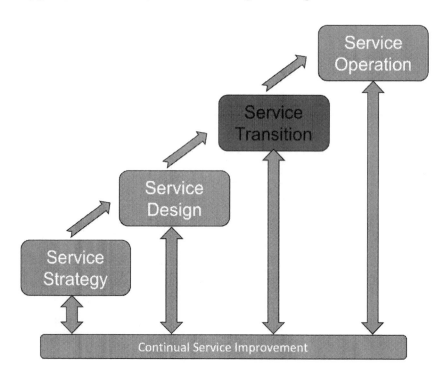

THE SERVICE V-MODEL

The **Service V-Model** defines progressive levels of activity and levels of testing/validation towards a defined objective, such as a release or major change. The testing that occurs at each level is imperative prior to moving to the next level in order to reduce overall risk during the implementation of a new or changed service.

As the stakeholders define the requirements and move down the Service V-Model, the service provider then moves up the right side of the model by conducting service validation and testing.

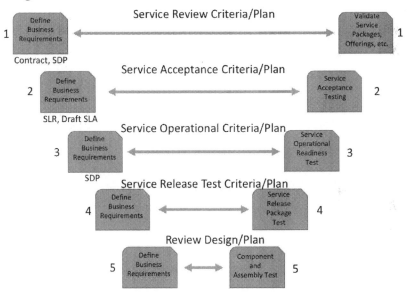

CHANGE MANAGEMENT PROCESS

The **Change Management Process** controls the lifecycle of all changes in order to enable beneficial changes to be made with a minimal disruption of IT services. It is concerned with recording, evaluating, approving, testing, and reviewing changes to services, systems, and other configuration items.

What is change? **Change** is the addition, modification, or removal of anything that could have an effect on IT services. Remember that all changes involve risk!

To initiate a change in the Change Management Process, a Request for Change (RFC) must be submitted. A **Request for Change** (RFC) is a documented request to alter a service or other Configuration Item (CI). RFCs are issued by customers, IT staff, users, or others, and are received by the Service Desk.

After the change is initiated by an RFC, it flows through a series of activities including the recording of the RFC, a review of the RFC, and assessment and evaluation of the RFC, the authorization of the RFC, planning, implementation coordination, review, and closure.

Changes come in three varieties: normal, standard, and emergency. A **normal change** is one that has a uniqueness to them that represents a higher risk or uncertainty of outcome. This is the default type of change that occurs, whereas emergency and standard are variations on the normal change procedures. An example of a normal change is when a new server or service is added to the live environment.

A **standard change** is a typical day-to-day change that is low-risk and well understood. These changes utilize a shorter version of the normal change procedures and minimizes the bureaucracy involved in order to quickly satisfy the customer's needs. An example of a standard change is when a user requests to move their workstation from one office to a new office in the same building.

An **emergency change** addresses unforeseen operational issues, such as failures, security threats, and vulnerabilities. This type of change is a rapid change that is required to continue the business operations. Emergency changes should still follow documented procedures and use the organizational Emergency Change Management process.

All changes must be properly authorized by someone with the appropriate level of authority. For the ITIL® v3 Foundation exam, you should be aware of three specific authorities for change: Change Manager, Change Advisory Board (CAB), and Emergency Change Advisory Board (ECAB).

The **Change Manager** is the protector and enforcer of the standards and processes to ensure positive change. They are responsible for ensuring that all change authorities have approved the changes before he makes the final approval. His role is to ensure good governance and to provide the final approval on all RFCs.

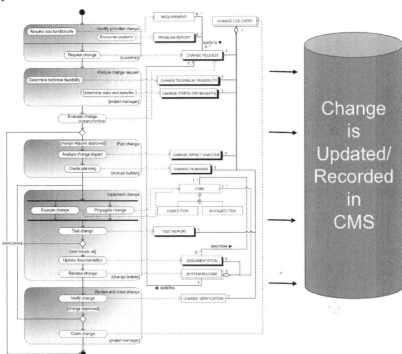

The **Change Advisory Board** (CAB) is responsible for providing a go/no-go decision for all changes. This group should meet on a regular basis (i.e. weekly). In large organizations, there may be many smaller CABs, but one is always the final decision maker for all changes.

The **Emergency Change Advisory Board** (ECAB) is a special group convened by the Change Manager to advise on the approval/rejection and planning for an emergency change. The membership of the ECAB includes people with experience and authority to make rapid, risk-based decisions. Even after the ECAB approves a change and the change is implemented, it is important for the normal change process to be revisited for the change to ensure that all the appropriate documentation has been updated.

Part of the Change Management Process is the development of change models for utilization by the organization. A **change model** is a group of predefined steps, procedures, and guidelines taken to handle a certain type of change. While there may be numerous change models that exist, there should only be one for each configuration item. These change models are used to help minimize risk, save costs, and improve the consistency of executing changes in the organization.

Change models can be either simple or complex. Simple change models are used for tasks like changing a password or moving a workstation. Complex change models are used for tasks like major system rollouts or large-scale configuration changes to the live environment.

RELEASE AND DEPLOYMENT MANAGEMENT PROCESS

The **Release and Deployment Management Process** is responsible for the planning, scheduling, and controlling the build, test, and deployment of releases. The process is also responsible for the delivery of new functionality required by the business while protecting the integrity of existing services. The release and deployment schedule is based upon the technical and business criteria of the organization.

A **release** is one or more changes to an IT service that are built, tested, and deployed together to achieve an objective. Each release consists of software, hardware, configurations, or a combination of these.

A **release unit** is a particular set of configuration items released together for a specific deployment effort.

SERVICE ASSET AND CONFIGURATION MANAGEMENT PROCESS

The **Service Asset and Configuration Management** (SACM) Process ensures that assets needed to deliver services are managed, and accurate/reliable information about those services is available. Service Asset and Configuration Management is vital to the Knowledge Management process.

One of the major informational items in the Service Asset and Configuration Management process is the Configuration Items (CIs). **Configuration Items** (CIs) are the individual records in your Configuration Management Database (CMDB). Each CI is a component or service asset that needs to be identified and managed.

A **baseline** in configuration management is the documented and validated configuration of a component, system, or service. It is a snapshot of a particular configuration at a specific moment in time and acts as the starting point when new equipment arrives. Any changes from baseline must be documented to account for the differences in the service's design vice its operation. In Information Security, it is common practice to create baselines of each type of workstation or server to ensure proper configurations are maintained.

The **Configuration Management System** (CMS) is an essential set of tools, data, and information on the configurations of the components, systems, and services. It is part of the Service Knowledge Management System (SKMS) and each SKMS can only have one definitive CMS. The CMS includes information on incidents, service requests, changes, problems, releases, errors, and much more.

The **Definitive Media Library** (DML) is a secure storage area for authorized software versions for every configuration item, including the licensing information and documentation. Before each item is placed into the definitive media library, it must be quality checked for integrity and to ensure there is no malicious code attached to it.

SERVICE VALIDATION AND TESTING PROCESS

The **Service Validation and Testing Process** provides a separate and more focused support for testing of the service, its systems, and its components prior to release. By using the Service Validation and Testing process, higher levels of quality control can be achieved with less errors entering the live environment.

Testing is performed under both the Change Management and the Release & Deployment Processes. It is important to use different testers in the Service Validation and Testing process than the ones used in the Release & Deployment process in order to ensure compliance and proper validation. This system of checks and balances creates a higher quality service for release.

TRANSITION PLANNING AND SUPPORT PROCESS

The **Transition Planning and Support Process** provides broader support for large-scale transitions and releases. If your organization has a large volume of changes, it can be helpful to implement this as a separate process. For example, if the organization is about to enter a merger or acquisition, setting up a separate Transition Planning and Support Process could help meet additional business objectives more successfully than trying to use the current sets of processes.

EVALUATION PROCESS

The **Evaluation Process** provides support for post-release evaluation and confirmation of customer acceptance of new and changed services. If your organization has had a problem with customer acceptance in the past, it can be helpful to implement this as a separate process.

KNOWLEDGE MANAGEMENT PROCESS

The Knowledge Management Process provides support for the capture and effective publishing of knowledge during the Service Transition phase. Knowledge Management begins in Service Transition but also continues throughout the rest of the lifecycle. Knowledge Management is concerned with the transition of data into information, then into knowledge, and finally into wisdom. This is also known as the DIKW Model.

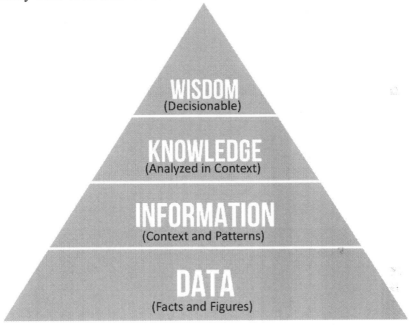

Data comes from many sources, such as configuration databases, service management tools, and even open-sources. The Service Knowledge Management System (SKMCS) contains all the data in a collection of repositories and systems. The Service Knowledge Management System also houses the Configuration Management Systems (CMS) and the CMS contain the Configuration Management Databases (CMDB).

Service Knowledge Management System (SKMS)

Contains CMS, service portfolios, service level agreements, capacity plan, user skill levels, technical documentation, and more

Configuration Management System (CMS)

Contains CMDBs and the tools used to manage themselves, the CMDBs, and the knowledge derived from these different tools

Configuration Management Database (CMDB)

Contains configuration item records for incidents, service requests, problems, known errors, changes, released, and more

Chapter 6
SERVICE OPERATIONS PHASE

OBJECTIVES

- Describe and understand the Service Operation phase
- Describe the principles of the Service Operation phase
- Describe the Incident Management Process
- Describe the Problem Management Process
- Describe the Event Management Process
- Describe the Service Request Fulfillment Process
- Describe the Access Management Process
- Describe the integration of Service Operations

The **Service Operations** phase begins upon transition of a new service to facilitate the outcomes desired by customers. All urgent operational problems are handled by this stage, while non-urgent problems are fed back to Service Strategy, Service Design, or Service Transition, as appropriate through the Continual Service Improvement process.

The Service Operations phase creates value by:
- Ensuring services are operated within expected performance parameters
- Restoring services quickly in the event of service interruption
- Minimizing the impact to the business in the event of service interruption
- Providing a focal point for communication between users and the Service Provider organization
- Having value realized by the customer by providing an operational service.

The Service Operations phase never really ends, but it does return to earlier stages for further development of the service in future revisions. During Service Operations, the service provider provides its users and customers with the agreed upon services and attempts to meet or exceed all service level agreements. Any faults are identified, quickly fixed, or referred back to an earlier stage for correction and implementation in a future version of the service.

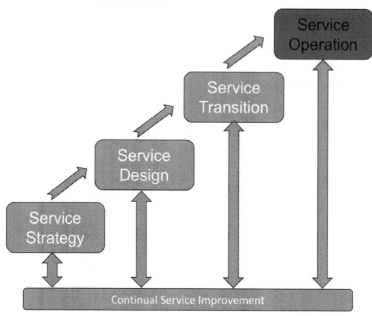

In the Service Operations phase, there are five processes we must learn: Incident Management, Problem Management, Event Management, Service Request Fulfillment, and Access Management.

PRINCIPLES OF SERVICE OPERATIONS

For effective and efficient service operations to occur, the service provider must ensure they seek out a proper balance and communicate with the key stakeholders.

The first essential principle of Service Operations is balance. There are four essential areas of concern when attempting to achieve a proper balance in information technology: internal information technology versus external business, stability versus responsiveness, cost versus quality, and proactive versus reactive. Each of these are a struggle for the IT Service Management organization, as each represents a cost of doing business, as well as a level of quality and support to their customers. Achieving the optimal balance to maximize value to the customer while minimizing the cost to the service provider is the continual challenge of IT Service Management.

The second essential principle of service operations is communication. Communication is critical in information technology operations. Whether the communication is between the service provider and its users/customers, or between operational teams/shift, there can never be enough communication in your IT Service Management organization. Communication with leadership through your performance reporting helps them make better decisions for the organization.

Within a given project or program, communication of issues early on can save time and money in the long term. Anytime a change, release, or deployment is planned, it must be communicated with both the end users and the support personnel to avoid a barrage of trouble tickets and service desk calls. Finally, when things go wrong (and they will), communicate the status of failures, exceptions, and emergencies so your customers know the current status and when you expect the issue to be resolved.

INCIDENT MANAGEMENT PROCESS

The **Incident Management Process** is responsible for restoring normal service operation as quickly as possible while minimizing the adverse impact on business operations, thereby ensuring the agreed upon level of service quality is maintained for the customer. This covers any event or occurrence that disrupts or may disrupt service delivery.

An **incident** is an unplanned interruption to an IT service, a reduction in the quality of an IT service, or failure of a configuration item (CI) that may impact service.

An **event** is any change of state of an infrastructure or other item which has significance for the delivery of a service.

A **problem** is the underlying cause of one or more incident, or even possible incidents (such as a warning).

A **workaround** is a method to minimize or eliminate the impact of an incident until a permanent fix can be implemented. For example, what would you do if a server loses power when an electrical breaker trips? You would most likely reset the breaker and restart the server. This may be a workaround. It didn't solve the root cause, or even determine why the breaker tripped originally, but you were able to restore services until a more permanent solution can be put into place.

A **known error** exists when you have an incident and a current workaround for that particular incident. This is not as good as a permanent solution, but it allows for the business operations to continue until a permanent solution can be developed and implemented. For example, assume that every time you turn on the toaster and the microwave at the same time in your office's break room, the circuit breaker trips causing a power outage. Your boss puts up a sign that says, "Don't use the microwave and the toaster at the same time!" Does this solve the problem for the long-term? No, but it is an example of an incident (power outages) and a workaround (don't use both devices at once). This becomes a known error. Eventually, an electrician will be called in to run a new outlet to the toaster, which will solve the problem permanently.

Every known error is stored in the **Known Error Database** (KEDB). This database forms part of the Configuration Management System (CMS) and details problems, workarounds, and known errors in a common database. It contains error records and problem records for easy searching and researching of issues.

INCIDENT MANAGEMENT PROCESS

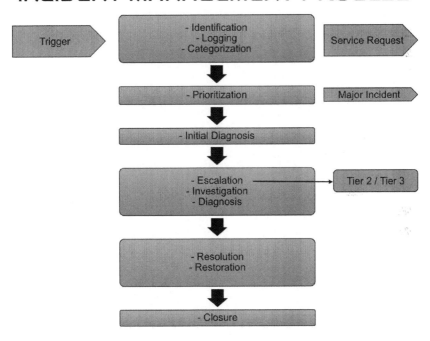

Detection/Identification occurs whenever a trigger happens. A trigger could be an exception detected during the Event Management process, a technician discovering an issue, the system auto-detecting an issue and creating a service ticket, or even as simple as a user calling the service desk to complain about an issue. Regardless of the trigger, the process has now begun because the issue has been detected or identified.

Logging is conducted by the Service Desk for all incidents. The Help Desk Analyst creates a ticket with as much detailed information as they can gather concerning the incident.

Classification/Categorization is performed by the Service Desk. Based on the categorization, the ticket is then pushed to the service request process or is treated as an incident per the incident management process in accordance with the Service Level Agreement.

Next, the incident is prioritized to ensure that service occurs based on triage of events and priority. The impact is determined based on the effect on the business and the urgency is weighed based on how long before impact is considered significant. Prioritization is based on the Service Level Agreement which determines the timeline to identify and resolve the incident. An example of a prioritization chart is provided in the following table:

PRIORITY	CATEGORY	TIME TO CORRECT
1	Critical	1 hour
2	High	4 hours
3	Medium	48 hours
4	Low	96 hours
5	When able	N/A

During Initial Diagnosis and Escalation, the Tier 1 Support performs triage on the incident. Can I fix this quickly? Do I need a specialist to solve this incident? Based on those questions, the Service Desk will either fix the issue or escalate the incident to a higher tier of support or a specialist. There are two forms of escalation: functional and hierarchal. **Functional escalation** is the most common type of escalation and occurs when an incident requires a specialist or skills beyond initial tier of Service Desk support. **Hierarchal escalation** occurs when an incident is referred to management due to the severity of the incident, the person affected by the incident, or needing special permission to obtain replacement components due to cost threshold the incident has created. Even after an incident is escalated, though, the Service Desk still owns the incident throughout its entire lifecycle.

Resolution and Recovery occurs once the investigation is complete and appropriate incident correction occurs. The solution to the incidents is reported back to the Service Desk and to the affected user.

Finally, closure is performed on the incident. You need to be careful not to close out an issue too early during closure, though. Just because the technician says the incident is fixed, doesn't mean the Service Desk can close the incident. First, the Service Desk should contact the end user and verify the fix has corrected their issue. If so, then the incident ticket can be closed and the details of what went wrong and how it was resolved should be documented in the incident ticket. Until the customer considers the issue resolved, the incident should not be closed.

PROBLEM MANAGEMENT PROCESS

The **Problem Management Process** focuses on the long-term solution and fixing the root cause of incidents. This is not the same as the Incident Management process, where the focus is often on firefighting and correcting issues as quickly as possible. The Problem Management Process is responsible for managing problems throughout their lifecycle, seeking to minimize the adverse impact of incidents and problems caused by underlying errors, and to prevent the recurrence of incidents related to those errors.

The Problem Management Process is triggered by the Incident Management, Problem Management, and the Event Management processes. It works to implement solutions through Change Management and the Release & Deployment processes to provide long-term solutions to recurring incidents.

There are two main types of problem management: reactive and proactive. **Reactive Problem Management** focuses on responding to problems as they arise in the environment and is triggered mainly by the incident management process. **Proactive Problem Management** focuses on seeking out improvements to service and infrastructure before an incident occurs. This is done mainly by working closely with the Availability Management and Capacity Management processes.

EVENT MANAGEMENT PROCESS

The Event Management Process works to manage the change of state that has significance for the management of a configuration item or service throughout its lifecycle. The lifecycle of an event is usually relatively short. There are three types of events: informational, warning, and exception.

An **informational event**, usually indicated as green, shows that everything is operating properly. For example, a successful logon by an authorized user or the completion of a server backup to an offsite data center may be logged as informational events. When an information event occurs, it is considered a completed event and is logged in the Configuration Management System (CMS).

A **warning event**, usually indicated as yellow, shows that something isn't operating properly. A warning indicates that a threshold has been breached and some actions should be taken before a failure occurs. For example, if the server's primary hard disk has reach over 80% capacity utilized, or the network utilization is over 85, a warning event may be logged. When a warning event occurs, it triggers the Problem Management Process to begin in order to determine the root cause and is logged in the Configuration Management System (CMS).

An **exception event**, usually indicated as red, shows that an error condition is occurring. An exception indicates that the current performance level is currently unacceptable. For example, if a failed login attempt occurs three times in a row, a software license has expired, or a backup server's network connectivity is no longer functional, an exception event may be logged. When an exception event occurs, it triggers the Incident Management Process or the Change Management Process to begin in order to resolve the issue.

SERVICE REQUEST FULFILLMENT PROCESS

The **Service Request Fulfillment Process** manages the lifecycle for all service requests from all users and delivers value directly and swiftly to users by enhancing their efficiency and effectiveness. This process also assists users in situations where no service degradation or interruption is involved.

Often, the users will try to circumvent the Service Request Fulfillment Process. As tempting as it may be to try to help these users circumvent the process, don't do it. In general, when a user circumvents the process to try and get service quicker, it usually ends up making the request take longer and aggravates both the user and the IT staff. Stick to the process, it works!

The Service Request Fulfillment Process is responsible for many different types of requests, including the creation of new user accounts, procurement and installation of new hardware, procurement and installation of new software, resetting a user's password, moving workstations from one office to another, and many other types of service requests.

Every request should be recorded in the Service Knowledge Management System as this can help in the Continual Service Improvement process. Each service request can trigger other processes, such as the Change Management, Incident Management, or Problem Management processes.

Remember, Service Request Fulfillment is about handling all requests, but not necessarily solving them for the users. After all, some requests that users will make are simply impossible to fulfill. Regardless, submit the request into the system and follow the process before issuing a rejection.

ACCESS MANAGEMENT PROCESS

The **Access Management Process** is responsible for providing the access rights to allow users to utilize a given service or group of services. The Access Management process simply executes the IT Security Policy set forth by the organization during the Information Security Management Process.

Some organizations do not treat access management as a separate process, but instead combine it into the Service Request Fulfillment, Change Management, or Release & Deployment processes, depending on their organizational design.

INTEGRATION OF SERVICE OPERATIONS

As discussed previously, many of the Service Operation phase processes are tightly integrated. For example, Event Management can trigger a Problem Management process, or a Service Request Fulfillment can trigger the Incident Management process.

Each is interwoven together by events, incidents, and problems, which form the core of the Service Operation phase workload. Consider the chart on the next page. While it may look very complicated at first, let us consider a few examples of how these processes are integrated in the real-world of service operations.

First, notice the dashed lines in the diagram, these represent processes outside of the Service Operations phase, but still interact with the Service Operations phase. For example, Change Management is a process in the Service Transition phase, but still receives inputs from the Service Operation processes and provides them input, as well.

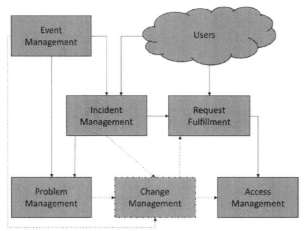

Let's consider the first example: A user calls the Service Desk with an issue which then creates an incident. This incident is more systemic, though, so it is categorized as a problem. This problem creates a workaround, becoming a Known Error, and eventually a solution is designed. To implement that solution, a change request is created, and once fielded, the problem is resolved and closed.

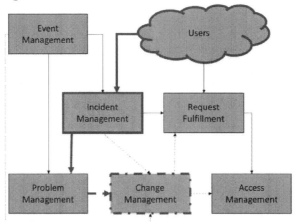

For our second example, consider that the IT Operations function is noticing that a large number of users are having issues logging into a particular service. The IT Operations team recommends that a problem is created. Once a solution is determined, they recommend a change through the Change Management process, which ultimately required access rights being changed for a particular user group, which is ultimately implemented by the Access Management process.

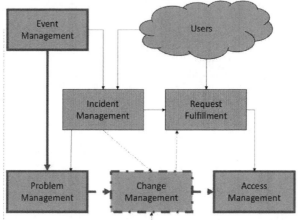

As you can see, these processes are quite integrated once the service is in the Service Operation phase. All of these processes and functions works together to provide the end users, our customers, with successful and efficient services in the Service Operation phase.

Chapter 7
CONTINUAL SERVICE IMPROVEMENT (CSI) PHASE

OBJECTIVES

- Describe and understand the Continual Service Improvement phase
- Describe measurements and metrics
- Describe the 7-Step Process Improvement Process
- Describe the Deming Cycle
- Describe the Continual Service Improvement Model
- Describe the role of automation in ITIL®

The **Continual Service Improvement** phase focuses on the alignment and realignment of services, processes, and functions to changing business needs. While it is most useful starting in the Service Operation phase, it does occur throughout all stages of the ITIL® v3 Lifecycle. By performing a strenuous Continual Service Improvement phase, IT Service Management organizations can identify processes and functions that need to be strengthened to increase efficiency.

The Continual Service Improvement (CSI) phase creates value to the business by ensuring services, processes, and other aspects of service management are aligned with business objectives. This phase is also focused on ensuring that services meet agreed upon performance levels, that efficiency of service delivery is always improving by minimizing cost, and that all aspects of the service management are undergoing constant reviews.

The main goal of the Continual Service Improvement phase is increasing efficiency. This is done by tracking customer issues, determining what issues keep occurring, determining what processes are failing, and what service agreements aren't working. All relevant information must be captured to inform appropriate fix actions by feeding back the information to earlier phases of the ITIL® v3 Lifecycle. Each inter-process link is verified as functional, effective, & efficient. Measurements and metrics are essential to performing Continual Service Improvement well, especially gathering and analyzing the service operations data.

The primary output of this phase is the Service Improvement Plan (SIP). The **Service Improvement Plan** (SIP) maps specific improvement objectives for an identified time period between one service review and the next service review. The Continual Service Improvement phase never really ends; in fact, you can even do Continual Service Improvement on the Continual Service Improvement phase itself!

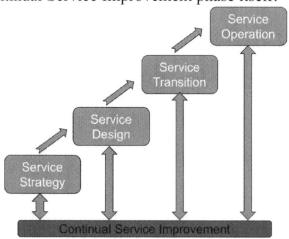

In the Continual Service Improvement phase, there is only one process that we must learn: the 7-Step Process Improvement Process.

MEASUREMENTS AND METRICS

In order to effectively improve your processes, it is important to have a method to quantifiably measure your success or failures. Measurements are useful to validate previous managerial decisions by providing evidence that we are performing the services correctly. Additionally, they can be used to direct activities by setting targets and determining if the Service Level Agreement targets are being met or exceeded.

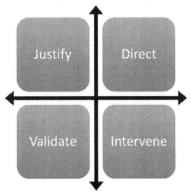

When a particular course of action is up for decision, measurements can provide evidence that a certain path is the correct one based on the facts and figures. Finally, measurements can be used to determine when an error needs to be corrected. For example, measurements can be useful to determine when a threshold is breached in Event Management and an incident or problem needs to be initiated. These four reasons for measurement can be summarized as justify, direct, validate, and intervene.

Management and decision makers love metrics. Sometimes, it seems like they simply cannot get enough of them. **Metrics** are measures that are captured and reported on for a given service, process, or activity. They are the baseline of measurement that is used in IT Service Management. There are three types of metrics: technology, process, and service.

Technology metrics measure components or application-based measurements, such as server availability or application performance.

Process metrics measure the process workflow through management tools.

Service metrics measure the end-to-end experience of a given service using service management tools.

These metrics then get rolled up into Key Performance Indicators (KPIs). A **Key Performance Indicator** (KPI) is a metric used to help manage an IT service, process, or activity, and is supported by metrics. KPIs can be either quantitative (measuring the amount of something) or qualitative (measuring the quality of something). The Key Performance Indicator is then rolled up into a Critical Success Factor (CSF).

The **Critical Success Factor** (CSF) is something that *must* happen for a service, process, or activity to succeed in its objectives. The CSFs are supported by its related KPIs.

The Objective establishes the reason for measurement in the first place. After all, measurements themselves have no value. A measurement's only value is to support the achievement of a specific objective.

Consider the example of providing email services that are available during business hours (the objective). It could be measured using the Critical Success Factor of the *Microsoft Exchange server must be available from 0800-1700 daily*. This Critical Success Factor is fed by one or more Key Performance Indicators, such as the one of maintaining 99.999% server uptime. This Key Performance Indicator could be fed by one or more metrics, such as Server Uptime, Bandwidth Utilization, etc.

MEASURING OBJECTIVES

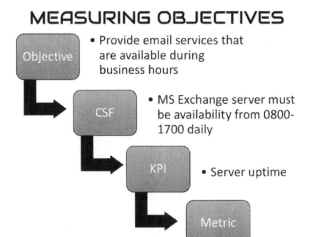

- Provide email services that are available during business hours

CSF
- MS Exchange server must be availability from 0800-1700 daily

KPI
- Server uptime

Metric

7-STEP PROCESS IMPROVEMENT PROCESS

The 7-Step Process Improvement Process forms the core of the Continual Service Improvement phase of the ITIL® v3 Lifecycle. It consists of seven basic steps:
1) Define the vision/strategy
2) Define what is to be measured
3) Gather the relevant data
4) Process the data for analysis in order for data to become information
5) Analyze the data for trends in order for information becomes knowledge
6) Leaders assess knowledge and produce service improvement plans
7) Implement the agreed upon changes

THE DEMING CYCLE

While the ITIL® v3 Foundation exam requires you to memorize the 7-Step Process Improvement Process steps, it also expects you to understand the Deming Cycle which heavily influenced the 7-Step Process Improvement Process' development. The Deming Cycle is an improvement model that found great success in the Japanese automobile manufacturing industry during the 20th century. The Deming Cycle is fairly simple, with only four steps being used: Plan, Do, Check, and Act.

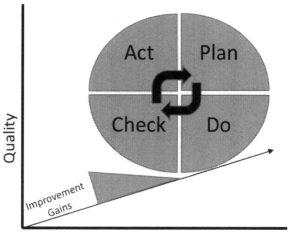

The Deming Cycle greatly influenced the 7-Step Process Improvement Process. In fact, a side-by-side comparison of the two shows just how neatly each of the seven steps bins into the four steps of the Deming Cycle:

DEMING CYCLE & 7-STEP

Deming	Step	Activity
Plan	1 2	• Identify vision, strategy, goals • Define what to measure
Do	3 4	• Gather data • Process data
Check	5 6	• Analyze data Present and use information
Act	7	• Implement changes

CONTINUAL SERVICE IMPROVEMENT MODEL

The final improvement model covered by the ITIL® v3 Foundation exam is called the Continual Service Improvement Model. This model is a simple set of guiding questions used to organize and perpetuate an improvement program within a service management organization. It also closely mirrors the ITIL® 7-Step Process Improvement Process. This model begins with the question *What is the vision* and ends with the question *How do we keep the momentum*, at which point process repeats the cycle by restarting and asking the questions again in an effort to continual improvement the service.

ROLE OF AUTOMATION IN ITIL

Unfortunately, humans can only focus on a few factors at once when making a decision in a complex situation. This is referred to as *bounded rationality*. Due to this human limitation, automation is important as it helps us to better understand the wide variety of factors that affect service management.

Automation is used to identify patterns and trends in large data sets, such as event logs, incident logs, and change requests. By using automation, decision makers can effectively confront complex scenarios, analyze large amounts of relevant data, and make the best decision possible.

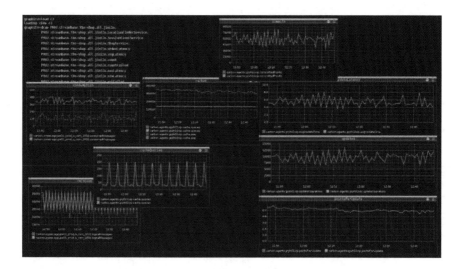

Automation can also aid in guaranteeing consistency during design phases of the lifecycle, utilizing toolsets like computer aided design (CAD), model and simulation, and other automation during the design phase. Another great use for automation is accurately recording high volumes of detailed data, such as incident logs and event logs. While computers are great at handling large data sets, people tend to make too many mistakes when compiling large amounts of data from various sources.

Back in the Incident Management process, we discussed the concept of prioritization. This is another area that automation can also assist the service management organization. Automation can be used to accurately prioritize incidents, problems, changes, and other issues, negating the human emotional components and relying on more rational decision making.

Finally, automation is necessary if the service management organization wishes to approach anything nearing a real-time response to issues and events. There is usually just too much data for a person to be able to manually parse through in a timely manner. By using automation instead, though, all of the problems, events, incidents, and logs can be correlated automatically, and the issues responded to in near real-time.

When considering how to successfully automate things inside your organization, you should always remember to define your processes accurately before any attempts are made to buy and apply an automation solution. Each process should be simplified to the maximum extent possible before attempting to automate those processes. Without efficiency of your processes, your automation will simply do the wrong thing more quickly!

Chapter 8
CONCLUSION

OBJECTIVES

- Be ready to take the ITIL® v3 Foundation certification exam

At this point, we have covered everything you need to know in order to take and pass the Information Technology Infrastructure Library (ITIL®) v3 Foundation certification exam. If you have read and understood everything you have read so far, you are almost ready to sit for the exam with confidence, and to pass it on your first attempt!

In this book, we covered all the essentials you need to know, with no fluff, filler, or extra material. Hopefully you have been able to learn the material quickly and are getting ready to conquer the certification exam with ease.

Now, before you go to schedule that certification exam, we just have one more thing to do to prepare: practice answering test questions. That's right, in this book, I have provided you with two full-length practice certification exams. Each practice exam is 40 questions long, just like the real exam. To get the maximum benefit from these exams, I recommend you find a quiet place to take them and time yourself for 60 minutes (just like the real exam).

Once you finish each exam, you will find all the answers and explanations listed in Appendix A (Practice Exam #1) and Appendix B (Practice Exam #2). Please take the time to go over each question and answer. If you missed a question, review the explanation and ensure you understand why the correct answer should have been chosen.

If you have read this entire book and took both practice exams scoring at least an 85% or higher, you will be ready to take and pass the ITIL® v3 Foundation exam on your first attempt!

Chapter 9
PRACTICE EXAM #1

GUIDELINES FOR THE PRACTICE EXAM

- Practice exams should be taken without using any notes
- Try to complete the 40 questions in under 60 minutes
- Aim to achieve a score of 85% or higher on this exam

1. What BEST describes a definitive media library (DML)?
    a) Secure location that holds definitive hardware spares
    b) Secure library where definitive authorized versions of all media configuration items (CIs) are stored and protected
    c) Database that contains definitions of all media CIs
    d) Secure library where definitive authorized versions of all software and back-ups are stored and protected

2. Service transition planning and support is NOT responsible for _____.
    a) Prioritizing conflicts for service transition resources
    b) Coordinating the efforts required to manage multiple simultaneous transitions
    c) Maintaining policies, standards, and models for service transition activities and processes
    d) Detailed planning of the build and test of individual changes

3. Service catalog management is NOT responsible for _____.
   a) Ensuring the service catalog contents are accurate
   b) Ensuring that service level agreements are maintained
   c) Ensuring that information in the service catalog is consistent with information in the service portfolio
   d) Ensuring that all operational services are recorded in the service catalog

4. What group should review any changes that must be implemented more quickly than can occur through the organization's normal change process?
   a) Technical management
   b) Emergency change advisory board
   c) Urgent change board
   d) Urgent change authority

5. What is the correct definition of an outcome?
   a) A result specific to the clauses in an SLA
   b) The result of carrying out an activity, following a process, or delivering an IT service
   c) All the accumulated knowledge of the service provider
   d) All incidents reported to the service desk

6. What function is responsible for managing a data center?
   a) Technical management
   b) Service desk
   c) Application management
   d) Facilities management

7. What document would you expect to see an overview of actual service achievements that your service is measured against achieving?
   a) Operational level agreement (OLA)
   b) Capacity plan
   c) Service level agreement (SLA)
   d) SLA monitoring chart (SLAM)

8. What is NOT an objective of service level management?
   a) Defining, documenting, and agreeing on the level of service to be provided
   b) Monitoring, measuring, and reporting of the actual level of service provided
   c) Monitoring and improving customer satisfaction
   d) Identifying possible future markets that the service provider could operate within

9. What BEST describes *partners* in the phrase "people, processes, products and partners"?
   a) Suppliers, manufacturers, and vendors
   b) Customers
   c) Internal departments
   d) The facilities management function

10. What DOES NOT provide value to the business during service strategy?
   a) Enabling the service provider to have a clear understanding of what levels of service will make their customers successful
   b) Enabling the service provider to respond quickly and effectively to changes in the business environment
   c) Reduction in the duration and frequency of service outages
   d) Providing a service with high utility and low warranty

11. What should a service *always* deliver to customers?
   a) Application
   b) Infrastructure
   c) Value
   d) Resources

12. What does NOT need to be defined as part of EVERY process?
   a) Roles
   b) Inputs and outputs
   c) Functions
   d) Metrics

13. What is it called when a service delivered between two business units in the same organization?
   a) Strategic service
   b) Delivered service
   c) Internal service
   d) External service

14. What statement about the service owner is INCORRECT?
   a) Carries out the day-to-day monitoring and operation of the service they own
   b) Contributes to continual improvement affecting the service they own
   c) Is a stakeholder in all of the IT processes that support the service they own
   d) Is accountable for a specific service within an organization

15. When can you raise or elevate a known error record?
   a) At any time it would be useful to do so
   b) After a workaround has been found
   c) Both A and B
   d) Neither A nor B

16. What is the BEST definition of IT service management?
    a) An internal service provider that is embedded within a business unit
    b) A complete set of all the documentation required to deliver world class services to customers
    c) Technical implementation of supporting IT infrastructure components
    d) The implementation and management of quality services that meet business needs

17. What BEST defines a customer-facing service?
    a) A service that directly supports the business processes of a customer
    b) A service that cannot be allowed to fail
    c) A service that is not covered by a service level agreement
    d) A service that is not directly used by the business

18. Who is responsible for carrying out activities in a process?
    a) Process owner
    b) Change manager
    c) Service manager
    d) Process practitioner

19. What process is used to compare the value that a newer service offers over one that is being replaced?
    a) Availability management
    b) Capacity management
    c) Service portfolio management
    d) Service catalog management

20. What BEST describes the purpose of the Service Operation stage in the service lifecycle?
   a) To decide how IT will engage with suppliers during the service lifecycle
   b) To proactively prevent all outages to IT services
   c) To design and build processes that meet business needs
   d) To deliver and manage IT services at agreed-upon levels to business users and customers

21. What key output is handed over to the service transition team at the end of the service design phase?
   a) Measurement, methods, and metrics
   b) Service design package
   c) Service portfolio design
   d) Process definitions

22. What do service metrics measure?
   a) Functions
   b) Maturity and cost
   c) End-to-end service
   d) Infrastructure availability

23. What process would seek to understand levels of customer satisfaction and communicate any plan of action that has been put in place to deal with dissatisfaction?
   a) Availability management
   b) Capacity management
   c) Business relationship management
   d) Service catalog management

24. What statement below is NOT true concerning the ITIL® framework and its worldwide adoption by many organizations?
   a) It is vendor-neutral
   b) It does not prescribe actions
   c) It represents best practices
   d) It is a proprietary framework

25. The effective management of risk requires specific types of action. What action would BEST manage risk?
    a) Training all staff how to identify and manage risk
    b) Identification and analysis of risk; management of the organization's exposure to risk
    c) Control of exposure to risk; investment of capital
    d) Training of all staff; investment of capital

26. What basic concepts are used in access management?
    a) Personnel, electronic, network, emergency, identity
    b) Rights, access, identity, directory services, service and service components
    c) Physical, personnel, network, emergency, service
    d) Normal, temporary, emergency, personal, group

27. What process is responsible for recording the current details, status, interfaces, and dependencies of all services that are being run or being prepared to run in the live environment?
    a) Service level management
    b) Service catalog management
    c) Demand management
    d) Service transition

28. What process includes business, service, and component sub-processes?
    a) Capacity management
    b) Incident management
    c) Service level management
    d) Financial management

29. What is NOT an objective of problem management?
    a) Minimizing the impact of incidents that cannot be prevented
    b) Preventing problems and incidents from occurring
    c) Eliminating recurring incidents
    d) Restoring normal service operation as soon as possible

30. What event categories are described in Service Operation?
    a) Informational, scheduled, normal
    b) Scheduled, unscheduled, emergency
    c) Informational, warning, exception
    d) Warning, reactive, proactive

31. What process or function is responsible for monitoring activities and events in the IT infrastructure?
    a) Service level management
    b) IT operations management
    c) Capacity management
    d) Incident management

32. What is NOT an aim of the change management process?
    a) To ensure the impact of changes are understood
    b) To ensure that changes are recorded and evaluated
    c) To ensure that all changes to configuration items (CIs) are recorded in the Configuration Management System
    d) To deliver and manage IT services at agreed-upon levels to business users

33. What activity is NOT performed by a service desk?
    a) Logging details of incidents and service requests
    b) Providing first-line investigation and diagnosis
    c) Restoring service
    d) Implementing all standard changes

34. What is TRUE about incident reporting and logging?
    a) Incidents can only be reported by users
    b) Incidents can be reported by anyone who detects a disruption or potential disruption to normal service
    c) All service desk calls must be logged as incidents
    d) Incidents reported by technical staff must also be logged as problems

35. Service design emphasizes the importance of the "Four Ps". This includes Partners, People, Processes and _____.
   a) Profit
   b) Preparation
   c) Products
   d) Potential

36. What stage of the service lifecycle is MOST concerned with defining policies and objectives?
   a) Service Design
   b) Service transition
   c) Continual improvement
   d) Service operation

37. What two processes contribute MOST to enabling effective problem detection?
   a) Incident and financial management
   b) Change and release and deployment management
   c) Incident and event management
   d) Knowledge and service level management

38. What process or function utilizes personnel to monitor events in an operation's bridge or network operations center?
   a) Technical management
   b) IT Operations Management
   c) Request fulfillment
   d) Applications management

39. Which database records all possible service improvements?
   a) CSI Register
   b) Known error database
   c) Capacity management information system
   d) Configuration Management database

40. What type of communication should functions utilize within service operation stage?
   a) Communication between data center shifts
   b) Communication related to changes
   c) Performance reporting
   d) Routine operational communication

Chapter 10
PRACTICE EXAM #2

GUIDELINES FOR THE PRACTICE EXAM

- Practice exams should be taken without using any notes
- Try to complete the 40 questions in under 60 minutes
- Aim to achieve a score of 85% or higher on this exam

1. What is the purpose of service transition planning & support?
   a) Provide overall planning for service transitions and coordinate the resources they require
   b) Ensure that all service transitions are properly authorized
   c) Provide the resources to allow all infrastructure elements of a service transition to be recorded and tracked
   d) Define test scripts to ensure transitions are unlikely to fail

2. What is the BEST description of the change authority, *change manager*, and *change advisory board*?
   a) Job descriptions
   b) Functions
   c) Teams
   d) Roles, people, or groups

3. Which processes are in the Service Transition stage?
   a) Change management, service asset and configuration management, release and deployment management
   b) Change management, capacity management, event management, service request management
   c) Service level management, service portfolio management, service asset and configuration management
   d) Service asset and configuration management, release and deployment management, request fulfillment

4. What is NOT a service desk organizational structure?
   a) Local Service Desk
   b) Virtual Service Desk
   c) IT Help Desk
   d) Follow the Sun

5. Whose responsibility is it to define metrics for change management?
   a) Change management process owner
   b) Change advisory board (CAB)
   c) Service owner
   d) Continual service improvement manager

6. What part of the lifecycle focuses on finding ways to improve process efficiency and cost effectiveness?
   a) Service operation
   b) Service transition
   c) Continual service improvement
   d) Service strategy

7. What is NOT a function of the service design stage?
   a) Designing and maintaining all necessary service transition packages
   b) Producing quality, secure, and resilient designs for new or improved services
   c) Taking service strategies and ensuring they are reflected in the service design processes and the service designs that are produced
   d) Transitioning a service from service design into service operations

8. Who is responsible for the definitive media library?
   a) Facilities management
   b) Access management
   c) Request fulfillment
   d) Service asset and configuration management

9. What is the BEST description of the relationships involved in the service asset and configuration management process?
   a) Describes the topography of the hardware
   b) Describes how the configuration items (CIs) work together to deliver the services
   c) Defines which software should be installed on a particular piece of hardware
   d) Defines how version numbers should be used in a release

10. What problem management activity ensures that problems can be tracked, and the information correlated by management?
   a) Categorization
   b) Detection
   c) Prioritization
   d) Escalation

11. What role is accountable for the operational management of a process?
   a) Process practitioner
   b) Process manager
   c) Service manager
   d) Change manager

12. What lifecycle stage's driving principle is creating value?
   a) Continual service improvement
   b) Service strategy
   c) Service design
   d) Service transition

13. What BEST describes the result of carrying out an activity, following a process, or delivering an IT service?
   a) Outcome
   b) Incident
   c) Change
   d) Problem

14. What process is responsible for discussing reports with customers and showing whether services met their targets?
   a) Continual service improvement
   b) Change management
   c) Service level management
   d) Availability management

15. What body exists to support the authorization of changes and to assist change management in the assessment and prioritization of changes?
    a) Change authorization board
    b) Change advisory board
    c) Change implementer
    d) Change manager

16. What group of people have an interest in the activities, targets, resources, and deliverables from service management?
    a) Employers
    b) Stakeholders
    c) Regulators
    d) Accreditors

17. What is the BEST definition of an event?
    a) Any change of state that has significance for the management of a configuration item or IT service
    b) An unplanned interruption to an IT service or a reduction in the quality of an IT service
    c) The unknown cause of one or more incidents that have an impact on an if service
    d) Reducing or eliminating the cause of an incident or problem

18. The implementation of ITIL® service management requires preparation and planning to effectively and efficiently use "the four Ps." What are these four Ps?
    a) People, process, partners, performance
    b) Performance, process, products, problems
    c) People, process, products, partners
    d) People, products, perspective, partners

19. What activity is conducted during the "Where do we want to be" step of the Continual Service Improvement (CSI) model?
   a) Implementing service and process improvements
   b) Reviewing measurements and metrics
   c) Creating a baseline
   d) Defining measurable targets

20. What CANNOT be provided by a tool?
   a) Knowledge
   b) Information
   c) Wisdom
   d) Data

21. Which stage of the service lifecycle should the processes necessary to operate a new service be defined?
   a) Service design - Design the processes
   b) Service strategy - Develop the offerings
   c) Service transition - Plan and prepare for deployment
   d) Service operation - IT operations management

22. What are the three service provider business models?
   a) Internal service provider, outsourced 3rd party, and off-shore party
   b) Internal service operations provider, external service operations provider, shared service unit
   c) Internal service provider, external service provider, outsourced 3rd party
   d) Internal service provider, external service provider, shared service unit

23. What would be the next step in the continual service improvement (CSI) model after "Did we get there"?
   a) What is the return on investment (ROI)?
   b) How much did it cost?
   c) How do we keep the momentum going?
   d) What is the value on investment (VOI)?

24. What step of the continual service improvement (CSI) model is BEST described by the phrase "Understand and agree on the priorities for improvement based on a deeper development of the principles defined in the vision"?
   a) Where are we now?
   b) Where do we want to be?
   c) How do we get there?
   d) Did we get there?

25. Where should details of a workaround be documented?
   a) Service level agreement (SLA)
   b) Problem record
   c) Availability management information system
   d) IT service continuity plan

26. What is an enabler of best practices?
   a) Standards
   b) Technology
   c) Academic research
   d) Internal experience

27. What process is involved in monitoring an IT service, and detecting when the performance drops below acceptable limits?
   a) Service asset and configuration management
   b) Event management
   c) Service catalog management
   d) Problem management

28. What is NOT an objective of request fulfillment?
    a) To provide information to users about what services are available and how to request them
    b) To update the service catalog with services that may be requested through the service desk
    c) To provide a channel for users to request and receive standard services
    d) To source and deliver the components of standard services that have been requested

29. What is concerned with policy and direction?
    a) Capacity management
    b) Governance
    c) Service Design
    d) Service level management

30. Where would you expect incident resolution targets to be documented?
    a) Service level agreement (SLA)
    b) Request for change (RFC)
    c) Service portfolio
    d) Service description

31. Availability management is directly responsible for the availability of _____.
    a) IT services and components
    b) IT services and business processes
    c) Components and business processes
    d) IT services, components, and business processes

32. What process will perform risk analysis and review of all suppliers and contracts on a regular basis?
    a) Service level management
    b) IT service continuity management
    c) Service catalog management
    d) Supplier management

33. What stage of the ITIL® lifecycle contains detailed descriptions of service catalog management, information security management, and supplier management?
    a) Service strategy
    b) Service design
    c) Service transition
    d) Service operation

34. What is NOT one individual aspects of service design?
    a) Design of the service portfolio and the service catalog
    b) Design of new or changed services
    c) Design of market spaces
    d) Design of the technology architectures

35. What BEST describes the act of transforming resources and capabilities into valuable service?
    a) Service management
    b) Incident management
    c) Resource management
    d) Service support

36. What is the BEST description of a major incident?
    a) Incident that is complex and requires a root cause analysis before a workaround can be developed
    b) Incident that requires many people to resolve
    c) Incident logged by a senior manager
    d) Incident that are classified as high priority or would have a high business impact

37. What is the BEST description of a service request?
    a) Request from a user for information, advice, or for a standard change
    b) Anything that the customer wants and is prepared to pay for
    c) Any request or demand that is entered by a user via a self-help web-based interface
    d) Any request for change (RFC) that is low-risk and which can be approved by the change manager without a change advisory board (CAB) meeting

38. What event categories are covered in service operations?
    a) Informational, scheduled, normal
    b) Scheduled, unscheduled, emergency
    c) Informational, warning, exception
    d) Warning, reactive, proactive

39. What would NOT commonly be discussed by the CAB?
    a) Details of failed changes
    b) Updates to the change schedule
    c) Reviews of completed changes
    d) All of these options

40. What type of baseline captures the structure, contents, and details of the infrastructure and represents a set of items that are related to each other?
    a) Configuration baseline
    b) Project baseline
    c) Change baseline
    d) Asset baseline

APPENDIX A:
ANSWER KEY TO PRACTICE EXAMS #1

OBJECTIVES

- Understand the correct answers to Practice Exam #1

As you check the answers to your Practice Exams #1, it is important to understand why each answer is correct. As you go over your practice exam results, ensure you pay close attention to the questions you missed and understand the explanation provided for their correct answers.

ANSWERS TO PRACTICE EXAM #1

1. **B** - Although the DML is a single logical store, it can be comprised of many physical locations including electronic storage areas. Its contents must be recorded in the CMDB and it is used heavily in Release and Deployment Management.

2. **D** - Service Transition is concerned with management of change, and more specifically, with the introduction of new and changed services into the live environment. Service Transition Planning is the process that oversees this lifecycle phase.

3. **B** - SLAs are maintained by the Service Level Agreement Management process, not the Service Catalog Management process.

4. **B** - In most environments, Emergency Changes are those which cannot be foreseen. Emergency Changes that are not addressed quickly put the environment at a high risk of experiencing a negative business impact. Emergency Changes are reviewed by the Emergency Change Advisory Board (ECAB).

5. **B** - The outcome is the result of carrying out an activity, following a process, or delivering an IT service. It refers to the intended or actual results.

6. **D** - Facilities Management is concerned with maintenance of the facilities which house IT operations, e.g. data centers, call centers, development facilities, etc.

7. **D** - SLAM charts provide an attractive, visual representation of achievement against targets of an SLA. Also known as stoplight charts, or Red-Yellow-Green charts.

8. **D** - Service Level Management is the process charged with securing and managing agreements between customers and the service provider regarding the levels of performance (utility) and levels of reliability (warranty) associated with specific services.

9. **A** - Partners are third-parties who provide services required to support the services. These include suppliers, manufacturers, and vendors.

10. **C** - The duration and frequency of service outages would be more associated with Availability Management or Problem Management than service strategy.

11. **C** - A service is a means of delivering value to customers by facilitating the outcomes customers want to achieve without the ownership of specific costs and risks. It is about delivering value to the customers!

12. **C** - Functions are self-contained subsets of an organization that are intended to accomplish specific tasks. They are not required for EVERY process.

13. **C** - This is called an internal service, and the service provider is called a Type I or Type II service provider.

14. **A** - The service owner is accountable for the overall design, performance, integration, improvement, and management of a single service.

15. **C** - A Known Error record is one that has an identified underlying cause and a workaround. It can be elevated or raised any time it would be useful to do so, or after a workaround has been found.

16. **D** - Service Management is a set of specialized capabilities for delivering value to customers in the form of services. ITIL® is a framework for IT Service Management.

17. **A** - Customer-facing is an adjective used to describe a hardware or software product, technology, or anything that the customer of a business deals with directly. It generally supports the business processes of the customer directly.

18. **D** - A Process Practitioner carries out one or more activities of a process and works with other stakeholders to ensure all contributions to the process are effective.

19. **C** - Service Portfolio Management process is concerned with management of the information concerning services in the Service Portfolio. It organizes the process by which services are identified, described, evaluated, selected, and chartered.

20. **D** - The Service Operation phase of the Service Lifecycle is concerned with ensuring that services operate within agreed parameters. When service interruptions do occur, Service Operation is charged with restoring service as quickly as possible, and with minimizing the impact to the business.

21. **B** - The Service Design Package is a comprehensive and high-quality package of documents that is passed from Service Design to Service Transition during the change in lifecycle phase.

22. **C** - Service metrics dictate what will be measured and how it will be measured. The most useful metrics will attempt to measure the end-to-end service experience.

23. **C** - Business Relationship Management is concerned with the relations at a high management level between service provider and the customer.

24. **D** - ITIL® is a public framework and does not contain proprietary information. This is one reason for its wide-spread adoption and success in the marketplace.

25. **B** - The identification and analysis of risk, as well as the management of risk exposure, is important to effectively manage risk during the delivery of services.

26. **B** - The Access Management process is charged with is providing authorized parties with appropriate access to the service and information as specified in the Information Security Policy. This includes things like user rights, access, identity, services, etc.

27. **B** - Service Catalog Management involves management and control of the Service Catalog, which contains information about services currently available to customers for use. The Service Catalog Management process is included within the Service Design phase.

28. **A** - Capacity Management ensures cost-effective capacity exists at all times to meet or exceed agreed upon needs of the business per the SLAs. It is defined as the maximum throughput a service, system, or component can handle.

29. **D** - "Restoring normal service operation as quickly as possible" falls under Incident Management, not Problem Management.

30. **C** - Events are listed as three basic types: information (no action required), warning (approaching a threshold), or exception (exceeded a threshold).

31. **B** - IT Operations Management is concerned with the day-to-day maintenance of the IT infrastructure and the facilities which house it. It is divided into two sub-functions: Operations Control and Facilities Management.

32. **D** - Change Management is concerned with recording, evaluating, approving, testing, and reviewing changes to services, systems, and other Configuration Items. All changes involve risk.

33. **D** - Standard changes are handled by Service Request Fulfillment, not the Service Desk.

34. **B** - Any user, technician, or person affected by an incident can be the one to report it and begin the incident response process.

35. **C** – The Four P's are People, processes, products, and partners.

36. **A** - Service Design focuses on the design and planning of all aspects of the lifecycle including its processes. This includes defining the policies and objectives to be used during Service Transition, Service Operations, & Continual Service Improvement phases.

37. **C** - Incident Management is concerned with the rapid restoration of services and with minimization of impact to the business. Event Management is concerned with detection of events in the infrastructure and with selection of appropriate response actions.

38. **B** - IT Operations Management is concerned with the day-to-day maintenance of the IT infrastructure and the facilities which house it. It is divided into two sub-functions: Operations Control and Facilities Management.

39. **A** - The CSI Register exists to record all potential improvement opportunities, and every stakeholder should be encouraged to submit entries into it.

40. **D** - All of these options are useful forms of communication during the service operations phase of the lifecycle.

APPENDIX B:
ANSWER KEY TO PRACTICE EXAMS #2

OBJECTIVES

- Understand the correct answers to Practice Exam #1

As you check the answers to your practice exam, it is important to understand why each answer is correct. As you go over your practice exam results, ensure you pay close attention to the questions you missed and understand the explanation provided for their correct answers.

ANSWERS TO PRACTICE EXAM #2

1. **A** - Service Transition Planning and Support provides overall planning for service transitions, and coordinates the resources that they will require.

2. **D** - Roles are defined as collections of specific responsibilities and privileges. These can be held by a person or a group or people.

3. **A** - Service Transition phase contains Change Management, Service Asset & Configuration Management, Release & Deployment Management, Transition Planning & Support, Service Validation & Testing, Evaluation, and Knowledge Management.

4. **C** - IT Help Desk is a generic term and not an organizational structure like the Local Service Desk, Virtual Service Desk, and Follow-the-Sun models.

5. **A** - The Change Management Process Owner is accountable for the overall design, performance, integration, improvement, and management of the change management process, including the metrics.

6. **C** - Continual Service Improvement is about the alignment and re-alignment of services, processes, and functions to changing business needs. CSI is concerned with the consistent application of quality management methods to the service.

7. **A** - The creation of service transition packages occurs during the Service Transition phase of the ITIL® Lifecycle.

8. **D** - The Definitive Media Library (DML) is the responsibility of the Service Asset and Configuration Management (SACM) process.

9. **B** - The CMS stores records of Configuration Items in the Configuration Management Database (CMDB). The CMS/CMDB differs from a traditional asset database in that it also provides information regarding how Configuration Items are related to each other.

10. **A** - The incident is categorized according to predefined criteria for the purpose of facilitating diagnosis and prioritizing its handling relative to other incidents.

11. **B** - The process manager is accountable for the management and oversight of a given process.

12. **B** - Service Strategy is about the selection of services a Service Provider will offer to customers. This is focused on determining how best to provide value to a service provider's customers.

13. **A** - An outcome is the result of carrying out an activity, following a process, or delivery an IT service. An outcome is the intended or actual result.

14. **C** - Service level management works with the customer to prove that the SLAs have been met or achieved.

15. **B** - The Change Advisory Board, or CAB, is a group of experts convened by the Change Manager to advise on the approval/rejection and planning for a specific change. The membership of the CAB usually varies with the change under consideration.

16. **B** - Stakeholders can be customers, users, or even suppliers. Everyone working within every type of service provider is a possible stakeholder.

17. **A** - An Event is any change of state which has significance for the delivery of a service. Event Management mainly focuses on IT detecting and addressing issues at the infrastructure level and is most commonly a largely automated process.

18. **C** - People (Human resources), Processes (Service Management Processes), Products (Technology and other infrastructure), and Partners (Third-parties) which support the service.

19. **D** - Metrics are useful in determining where you currently are, and determining where you want to be, in terms of service levels during the Continual Service Improvement (CSI) phase.

20. **C** - Wisdom is correct, well-informed decisions based on accurate data that is analyzed and presented in the correct context.

21. **A** - Service Design focuses on the design and planning of all aspects of the lifecycle including its processes. This includes defining the policies and objectives to be used during Service Transition, Service Operations, & Continual Service Improvement phases.

22. **D** - There are three types of service providers. Type I (internal service provider embedded in the business unit), Type II (internal service provider shared among the business units), and Type III (external service provider).

23. **C** – "How do we maintain momentum?" Is the 6th step in the CSI process, and then the cycle repeats.

24. **B** - "Where are we now?" comes right after "What is the vision?".

25. **B** - The Problem Record would exist in the Known Error Database (KEDB), and it would be updated with a workaround once the error becomes a "known error".

26. **B** - Standards, academic research, and internal experience can be good sources of best practices, but technology is an enabler of best practices!

27. **B** - Event Management is concerned with detection of events in the infrastructure and with selection of appropriate response actions. It monitors things such as technical components, environmental conditions, software, and security CIs to ensure performance.

28. **B** - Service Request Fulfillment is the process charged with assisting users in situations where no service degradation or interruption is involved. It provides a means for common user requests for non-incident support, new equipment, training, etc.

29. **B** - Governance is concerned with policy and direction, and ensures we focus on conformance and compliance, especially compliance to legislative requirements like Sarbanes-Oxley, Freedom of Information, Data Protection, etc.

30. **A** - Service Level Agreements (SLAs) should specify service and quality targets, including those for incident resolution.

31. **A** - The Availability Management process is concerned with management and achievement of agreed availability requirements as established in Service Level Agreements. In ITIL®, availability is defined as the ability of a system, service, or configuration item to perform its function when required.

32. **D** - Supplier Management is the process charged with obtaining value for money from third-party suppliers. Supplier Management plays a very similar role to that of Service Level Management, but with respect to external suppliers.

33. **B** - Service Design contains Service Catalog Management, Service Level Management, Availability Management, Capacity Management, Service Continuity Management, IT Security Management, and Supplier Management.

34. **C** - The design of market spaces is part of Service Strategy, not Service Design.

35. **A** - Service Management is a set of specialized capabilities for delivering value to customers in the form of services. These services require resources and capabilities to operate.

36. **D** - A major incident has a high impact on the business or is affected a high priority customer.

37. **A** - Service requests can be anything request by a user, including service, help, advice, guidance, a standard change, or even a continual service improvement suggestion.

38. **C** - Events are classified as Informational (no action required), Warning (item is approaching a performance or capacity limitation), or Exception (item has exceeded a threshold).

39. **D** - The Change Advisory Board or CAB is a group of experts convened by the Change Manager to advise on the approval/rejection and planning for a specific change. The membership of the CAB usually varies with the change under consideration.

40. **A** - Configuration Baseline refers to the documented and validated configuration of a component, system, service, etc. and is used to provide a roll-back point useful in managing risk around changes in the environment.

APPENDIX C:
GLOSSARY OF TERMS

OBJECTIVES

- Provide a reference for key terms and definitions

Access Management Process
Responsible for providing the access rights to allow users to utilize a given service or group of services

Accountable
Person who owns the activity and must answer for its outcomes

Alternate View Service Catalogs
Service catalog that can be displayed in various formats to show the relationships between various retail customers, business-to-business, and technical or supporting service providers

Application Development
Focused on design and construction of application solutions to gain utility

Application Management
Provide end-to-end management of applications in the environment which involves cultivating the skill sets and resources to support all phases of the service lifecycle

Availability
Ability of a service, system, or configuration item to perform its function, when required

Availability Management Process
Concerned with meeting current and future availability needs of the business by ensuring that the level of availability delivered in all IT services meets the agreed availability needs and/or service level targets in a cost effective and timely manner

Baseline
Documented and validated configuration of a component, system, or service; a snapshot of a particular configuration at a moment in time

Best Practices
Proven activities or processes that have been successfully used by many different organizations in a specific industry

Budgeting
Forecasting and planning of how to spend money in relation to providing a service

Business Capacity Management
Aligns capacity management to business plans and strategy

Business Case Analysis
A structured and documented justification for a new investment that argues the benefits and costs of a particular service

Business or Customer Service Catalog
Identifies the business processes that are being supported by the services; detailed versions can include service hours, SLA info, escalation paths, etc.

Capabilities
Intangible items that contribute to a service

Capacity
Maximum throughput of a service, system, or configuration item

Capacity Management Process
Concerned with meeting current and future capacity and performance-related needs of the business; ensures the capacity of IT services and the IT infrastructure meets the agreed capacity and performance-related requirements in a cost-effective and timely manner

Centralized Service Desk
Makes better use of resources, improves consistency, and centralizes management

Change
Addition, modification, or removal of anything that could have an effect on Information Technology services

Change Advisory Board (CAB)
Focused on providing a go/no-go decision for all changes and meets on a regular basis (i.e. weekly)

Change Management Process
Controls the lifecycle of all changes in order to enable beneficial changes to be made with a minimal disruption of IT services

Change Manager
Protector and enforcer of the standards and processes to ensure positive change

Change Model
Predefined steps, procedures, and guidelines taken to handling a certain type of change

Charging
Getting payment from the customers for services

Commodity Suppliers
Involves provision of low-value products, such as printer ink or bathroom supplies

Component Availability
Focused on each individual piece that together provides the end-to-end experience

Component Capacity Management
Ensures an appropriate understanding of the technical components in the infrastructure by employing data analysis techniques to get maximum value from components

Confidentiality
Ensures only those with a "need to know" can access the information system or data held by the system

Configuration Items
The individual records in your Configuration Management Database (CMDB); a component or service asset that needs to be identified and managed

Configuration Management System (CMS)

An essential set of tools, data, and information on configurations; part of the Service Knowledge Management System (SKMS) that includes information on incidents, service requests, changes, problems, releases, errors, and much more

Consulted

The person who reviews and provides advice and authorization for the activity in the RACI Model

Continual Service Improvement (CSI)

Focuses on the alignment and realignment of services, processes, and functions to changing business needs

Critical Success Factor (CSF)

Something that must happen for a service, process, or activity to succeed in its objectives

Definitive Media Library (DML)

A secure storage area for authorized software versions for every configuration item, including the licensing information and documentation

Demand Management Process

Used to identify the demand for a particular service to prevent capacity limitations

Emergency Change

Address unforeseen operational issues, such as failures, security threats, and vulnerabilities

Emergency Change Advisory Board (ECAB)

A special group convened by the Change Manager to advise on the approval/rejection and planning for an emergency change

Evaluation Process
Provides support for post-release evaluation and confirmation of customer acceptance of new and changed services

Event
Any change of state of an infrastructure or other item which has significance for the delivery of a service

Exception Event
Usually indicated as red, this event shows that an error condition is currently occurring

Facilities Management
Concerned with physical environment of the IT infrastructure, including the power, cooling, fire suppression, and physical access to the data centers and server rooms.

Financial Management Process
Used to understand and manage financial resources, costs, and opportunities for a service

Follow-the-Sun Model
Combines local, centralized, and virtual service desks, allowing for 24x7 coverage across all time zones

Functional Escalation
Most common type of escalation; occurs when an incident requires a specialist or skills beyond initial tier of Service Desk support

Functions
Self-contained unit of an organization specialized to perform specific tasks and are responsible for an outcome

Hierarchal Escalation
Occurs when an incident is referred to management due to the severity of the incident, the person affected by the incident, or needing special permission to obtain replacement components due to cost threshold the incident has created

Incident
An unplanned interruption to an IT service, a reduction in the quality of an IT service, or failure of a configuration item (CI) that may impact a service

Incident Management Process
Responsible for restoring normal service operation as quickly as possible while minimizing the adverse impact on business operations, thereby ensuring the agreed upon level of service quality is maintained for the customer

Information Security Management Process
Aligns IT security with business security, ensuring the IT security aspects match agreed-upon needs of the business by protecting IT assets and services from security threats

Information Technology Infrastructure Library (ITIL®)
Developed as a framework for organizations to use in order to perform IT Service Management (ITSM)

Information Event
Usually indicated as green, it is an event that shows that everything is operating properly

Informed
The person who receives updates on activity's progress in the RACI Model

Integrity
Ensures that the data and services are complete, accurate, and unmodified

ISO 27000
International standard for Information Systems Management

IT Operations Management
Provides a stable platform on which services can be delivered to meet the agreed-upon business needs; performs the day-to-day running of the IT infrastructure and the facilities that house the infrastructure

IT Service Continuity Management Process
Ensures that the service provider can always provide the minimum agreed upon service levels by managing the risks associated with a disaster (or other incidents) that could seriously affect critical IT services

IT Service Management (ITSM)
Complete set of activities required to provide value to a customer through services, including policies and strategies to Plan, Design, Deliver, Operate, and Control IT services

Key Performance Indicator (KPI)
Metric used to help manage an IT service, process, or activity and is supported by metrics

Known Error
Exists when you have an incident and a current workaround for that particular incident

Known Error Database
Forms part of the Configuration Management System (CMS); details problems, workarounds, and known errors in a common database

Local Service Desk
Located physically close to the customers they support

Metrics
A measure that is captured and reported on for a given service, process, or activity

Normal Change
Change that has a uniqueness to them that represents a higher risk or uncertainty of outcome; this is the default type of change

Operational Level Agreement (OLA)
Underpinning written agreement between two elements of the service provider organization regarding key service targets and responsibilities of both parties for the services being supported

Operational Suppliers
Involves supply of operational services

Operations Control
Monitors the infrastructure for optimal performance minute-by-minute and conducts the normal maintenance cycles required

Partners
People and organizations that help the service provider provide excellent services

People
Consist of the technical staff, users, customers, stakeholders, board executives, and many others

Proactive Problem Management
Focuses on seeking out improvements to service and infrastructure before an incident occurs

Problem
Underlying cause of one or more incidents, or even possible incidents (such as a warning)

Problem Management Process
Problem Management focuses on the long-term solution and fixing the root cause

Process
Set of coordinated activities combining resources and capability to produce an outcome that creates value for the customer

Process Manager
Accountable for development, performance, and improvement of a process

Process Metrics
Measure the process workflow through management tools

Process Owner
Accountable for the overall design, performance, integration, improvement, and management of a single process

Process Practitioner
Responsible for actually conducting the actions and functions associated with operating the service

Processes
Set of coordinated activities combining resources and capability to produce an outcome that creates value for the customer; ITIL® v3 Lifecycle contains 26 distinct processes

Product Manager
Accountable for the development, performance, and improvement of a group of related services

Products
Made up of other services, technology (hardware, software, etc.), and tools needed to support the services

RACI Model
A generic tool for reviewing and assigning four key roles to any activity: Responsible, Accountable, Consulted, and Informed

Reactive Problem Management
Charged with responding to problems as they arise in the environment and is triggered mainly by the incident management process

Release
One or more changes to an IT service that are built, tested, and deployed together to achieve an objective; consists of software, hardware, configurations, or a combination of these

Release and Deployment Management Process
Responsible for the planning, scheduling, and controlling the build, test, and deployment of releases, as well as delivering new functionality required by the business while protecting the integrity of existing services

Release Unit
A particular set of configuration items released together for a specific deployment effort

Request for Change (RFC)
Documented request to alter a service or other Configuration Item (CI)

Resources
Tangible items that contribute to a service

Responsible
Role for the person who executes or performs the activity

Return on Investment (ROI)
The expected financial growth created by a service

Roles
A collection of specific responsibilities, duties, or positions within a process or function

Service
Means of delivering value to customers by facilitating the outcomes customers want to achieve without the ownership of specific costs and risk

Service Asset and Configuration Management
Ensures that assets needed to deliver services are managed and accurate/reliable information about them is available

Service Assets
Resources and capabilities which the service provider must allocate to provide a given service

Service Availability
Focused on end-to-end service that is experienced by the end user or customer

Service Capacity Management
Ensures services underpin the business processes and outcomes by focusing on end-to-end performance of operational services and workloads

Service Catalog
A database or structured document with information about all live services including those available for deployment that it is widely available to those who are approved to access it

Service Catalog Management Process
Involves management and control of the Service Catalog

Service Desk
Provides a single, central point of contact for all users of IT services

Service Improvement Plan (SIP)
Primary output of the periodic service reviews conducted as part of the CSI process; maps specific improvement objectives for an identified time period between one service review and the next service review

Service Level Agreement (SLA)
Written agreement between IT service provider and customer providing key service targets and responsibilities of both parties

Service Manager
Accountable for development, performance, and improvement of a service

Service Metrics
Measure the end-to-end experience of a given service using service management tools

Service Operations
Begins upon transition of a new service to facilitate the outcomes desired by customers; Urgent operational problems are handled by this stage while non-urgent problems are fed back to Service Strategy, Service Design, or Service Transition, as appropriate

Service Owner
Accountable for the overall design, performance, integration, improvement, and management of a single service

Service Portfolio
Complete set of services under management by a service provider

Service Portfolio Management Process
Process concerned with managing the services that comprise the service portfolio

Service Request Fulfillment Process
Manages the lifecycle for all service requests from all users and delivers value directly and swiftly to users by enhancing their efficiency and effectiveness

Service Strategy
Establishes and manages the broadest policies and standards to govern how a Service Provider will operate

Service Transition
Conducts the management of change, and more specifically, the introduction of new and changed services into the live environment

Service V-Model
Defines progressive levels of activity and levels of testing/validation towards a defined objective such as a release or major change

Service Validation and Testing Process
Provides separate and more focused support for testing of the service, its systems, and its components prior to release

Simple Service Catalog
Simplified matrix of available services with comprehensive and accurate information on those services

Standard Change
A typical day-to-day change that is low-risk and well understood

Strategic Suppliers
Involves senior managers and sharing of confidential long-term plans

Strategy Management Process
Ensures a service strategy is defined, maintained, and managed

Supplier Management Process
Responsible for obtaining quality service from suppliers that provides fiscal value to meet the agreed upon needs of the business; ensures suppliers meet their contractual obligations

Tactical Suppliers
Involves significant commercial activity and business interaction

Technical Management
Responsible for the procurement, development, and management of the technical skill sets and resources required to support the infrastructure and the ITSM efforts

Technical or Supporting Service Catalog
Provides another level of depth to the service catalog by covering infrastructure, applications, and outsourced services

Technology Metrics
Measure components or application-based measurements, such as server availability or application performance

Transition Planning and Support Process
Provides broader support for large-scale transitions and releases

Underpinning Contract
Legally binding agreement that conform to contract law and organizational contract policy that is written in "legalese" by a lawyer

Utility
Fit for purpose of a given service

Value
Created from the balance between utility and warranty

Value on Investment (VOI)
The expected non-financial return created by a service, such as in a service provider's increased recognition or reputation

Virtual Service Desk
Does not require a centralized location, but still makes better use of resources, improves consistency, and centralizes management

Warning Event
Usually indicated as yellow, it is an event that shows that something isn't operating properly

Warranty
Fit for use of a given service

Workaround
Method to minimize or eliminate the impact of an incident until a permanent fix can be implemented

ITIL® v3 Foundations: Your Complete ITILv3 Exam Prep

This course is your complete guide to all 26 processes and functions covered by the ITILv3 Foundation certification exam. If you are interested in learning more about IT Service Management, this is the course for you! You will pass the exam on your first attempt **IF** you follow our methods and study using this course. Join us and get ITIL certified!

ITIL® v3 Foundations: Practice Certification Exams

This course gives you 6 full-length practice exams to prepare for the ITILv3 Foundation certification exam. If you want to practice the exam before you spend $150 for the certification exam fee, this is the course for you! Each exam is timed for 60 minutes and has 40 questions (just like the ITILv3 Foundation). Every question comes complete with the explanation of why each answer is correct, making it a great learning tool!

CompTIA CySA+ (CS0-001): Course & Practice Exam

In this course, you will receive over 10 hours of video teaching you everything you need to know to take and pass the CompTIA CySA+ certification exam, including a full-length practice exam. This course is simply outstanding. Check out the reviews from previous students, if you want to pass the CySA+ certification, join this course!

CompTIA Security+ Certification: Course & Practice Exam

This course teaches you everything you need to know to pass the Security+ certification exam, complete with hours of video lectures and hundreds of practice questions. Learn the fundamentals of security in this essential course to entering the cybersecurity career field.

CompTIA Network+ Certification: Course & Practice Exam

This course teaches you everything you need to know to pass the Network+ certification exam, complete with 8.5 hours of lecture and hundreds of practice questions. This course is the key to your success in passing the exam

Visit **http://www.DionTraining.com** for more details!
Follow us on Facebook: JasonDionTraining
Subscribe on YouTube: JasonDionTraining

ITIL® v3 Foundations: Cram to Pass

In this 3.5 hour video course, you will review everything covered in this book. This course is designed to get you ready to take and pass the ITIL® v3 Foundation certification exam in the next 7 days! This online video course also comes with 2 full-length practice exams. In just 30-60 minutes a day, you will be ready to conquer the exam on your first attempt!

ABOUT THE AUTHOR

Jason Dion, is an Adjunct Assistant Professor at the University of Maryland University College and an Adjunct Instructor at Liberty University's College of School of Business and Anne Arundel Community College's Department of Computing Technologies. He holds numerous information technology professional certifications, including Certified Information Systems Security Professional (CISSP), Cybersecurity Analyst+ (CySA+), CyberSec First Responder (CFR), Certified Ethical Hacker (CEH), Certified Network Defense Architect (CNDA), Digital Forensic Examiner (DFE), Digital Media Collector (DMC), Security+, Network+, A+, and Information Technology Infrastructure Library v3 Foundation.

With networking experience dating back to 1992, Jason has held positions as an IT Director, Deputy Director of a Network Operations Center, Network Engineer, and many others. He holds a Master of Science degree in Information Technology with a specialization in Information Assurance from University of Maryland University College, a Master of Arts and Religion in Pastoral Counseling from Liberty University, and a Bachelor of Science in Human Resources Management from New School University. He lives in the greater Washington D.C./Baltimore, Maryland area with his wife and two children.

71423797R00080

Made in the USA
Middletown, DE
23 April 2018